# ROADS TO RIDE

HEYDAY BOOKS

# Roads to Ride

A Bicyclist's
Topographic Guide
to Alameda,
Contra Costa and
Marin Counties

By
Grant Petersen
with
Mary Anderson

Dedicated to B.F. Skinner (who must be the most misunderstood person of all time) and Bob Dylan. It's the least I can do and the only thing I can think of.

Photographs: Matthew Wong

Design: Dennis Gallagher
and Sarah Levin

Editing: Karin Rosman

Cartography and Production:
Sarah Levin and Jenne Mowry

Copyright © 1984 by
Grant Petersen

Printed in the United States of America.
10 9 8 7 6 5 4 3

Published by
Heyday Books
Box 9145
Berkeley, California 94709

ISBN: 0-930588-07-x
Library of Congress Catalog
Card: 83-080352

# Acknowledgements

I want to thank a lot of people for the various degrees and types of help they provided. In no particular order, thank you Doug Matsumoto, for drawing, designing, driving, and advice Ken Bechtol, for driving Matthew Wong, for driving and photographing Olga Petersen—my grandmother—for supplying the car Rich Davies, for loaning me the altimeter Carl Petersen—my father—for driving and support Gary Zukav, for advice Nancy Ringler, for advice

Mark Schmidt, for advice and proofreading the text Tom Ritchey, frame builder Mary Anderson, for driving, organizing, reading, understanding, and encouraging Elizabeth Petersen—my mother —for encouragement, care Tim Parker, for reading early portions of the manuscript Other friends and co-workers who, with everyday questions like, "How's the book coming along?" kept me moving towards its completion The staff at Heyday Books, for their advice, criticism, and sparring, which helped make this a better book

Theresa Chiu and Jeanne Matlick for their kindness; Huret, for the Jubilee.

In Memory of
Eric Allen
May 17, 1958-November 15, 1979

Patterson Pass Rd.

# Contents

A sample road is diagrammed here to describe the notations used in this book.

## Sample Rd. (Map A, B, or C) [1]

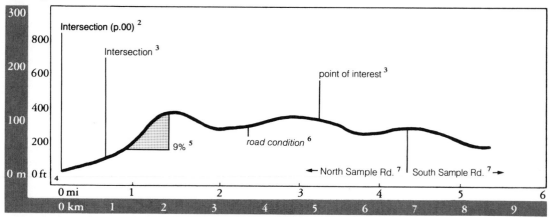

1. Alameda and Contra Costa Counties are portrayed in three overall maps, A, B, C (pages 13-15). The notation after the road name indicates on which map this road appears. All Marin County roads appear on the Marin County map (page 93).
2. Roads that are profiled elsewhere in the book are printed in bold letters. Page numbers indicate where in the book the roads appear.
3. Non-profiled roads and other landmarks or points of interest are printed in lighter letters.
4. "0 ft" is the lowest point on the road, and other elevations are relative to it. Elevations do not refer to feet above sea level.
5. Grades are given as percentages, not degrees. Thus 9% means that the road rises 9 feet for every 100 feet it travels.
6. Road conditions are printed in light italics.
7. When a road changes name, it is shown by a name plus an arrow, usually beneath the profile.

This is a book for people who like to ride bicycles but don't always know where to go. It's for riders who sometimes want a change of pace from their home roads, and who don't have lots of time to experiment. And, it's for riders who are already familiar with most of these roads and are interested in a more objective, comparative view of them.

These are profiles of most of the popular, useful, or interesting roads in Marin, Contra Costa, and Alameda Counties. The altitude data was obtained with an odometer and an altimeter (Thommen #2000). Many roads were recorded more than once and in opposite directions, and the results were reassuringly consistent. You can trust these profiles to provide you with reasonably accurate and useful representations of the ups and downs you'll be encountering.

The text in this book is trim. Detailed directions and lavish descriptions are more appropriate for travel brochures or when trying to persuade the reluctant to go for a ride. These brief descriptions may require a greater sense of adventure, but they allow for more discovery.

*How to use this book:* The book is divided into two sections— East Bay (pages 11-89) and Marin (pages 91-137). At the beginning of each section are overall maps; profiles of individual roads follow in alphabetical order. To use this book, first plot out a trip on one of the overall maps. Then look up the individual road profiles for details on topography and road conditions. (If you have trouble finding a particular road, please refer to the index at the back of the book.) By working back and forth between the overall maps and the individual profiles, you can devise a trip closely suited to your needs.

Bear Creek Rd.

# Alameda and
# Contra Costa Counties

Wildcat Canyon Rd.

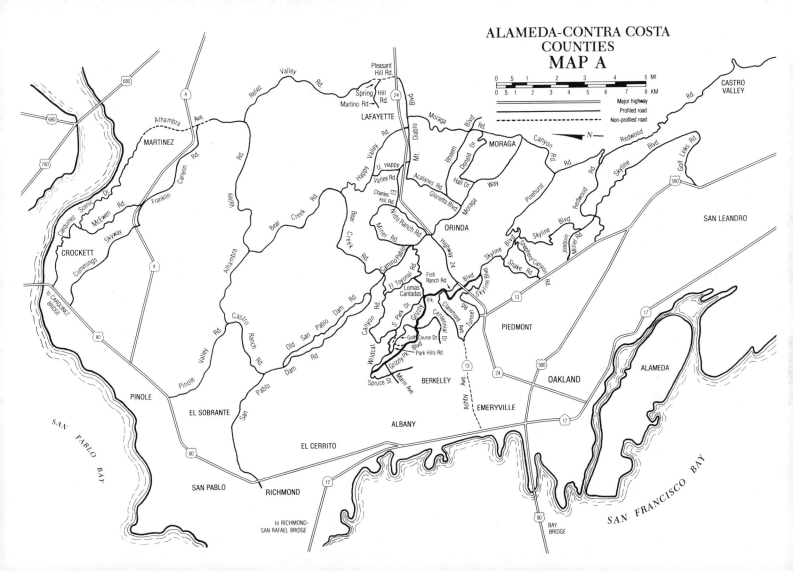

ALAMEDA-CONTRA COSTA
COUNTIES
MAP A

| 0 | .5 | 1 | | 2 | 3 | 4 | 5 MI |

Major highway
Profiled road
Non-profiled road

N→

CASTRO VALLEY

SAN LEANDRO

SAN PABLO BAY

CROCKETT

MARTINEZ

LAFAYETTE

MORAGA

ORINDA

PIEDMONT

OAKLAND

ALAMEDA

PINOLE

EL SOBRANTE

BERKELEY

EMERYVILLE

ALBANY

EL CERRITO

SAN PABLO

RICHMOND

SAN FRANCISCO BAY

BAY BRIDGE

to RICHMOND-
SAN RAFAEL BRIDGE

to CARQUINEZ
BRIDGE

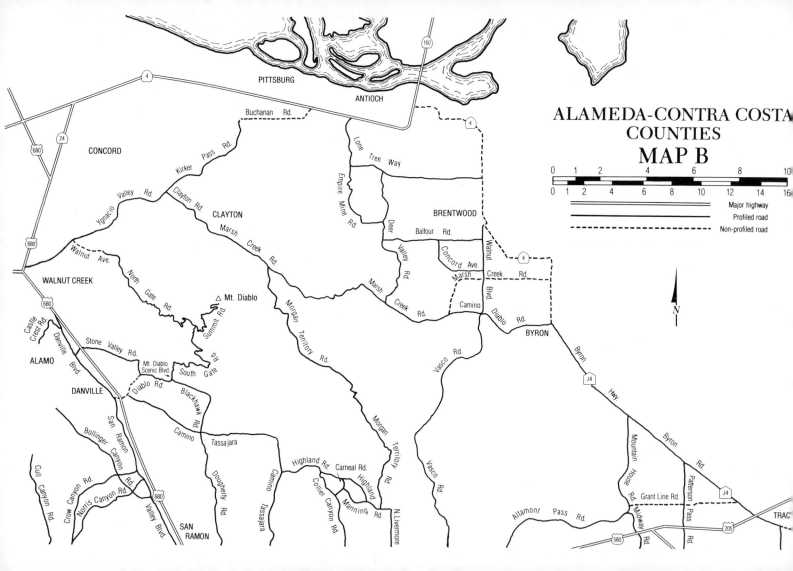

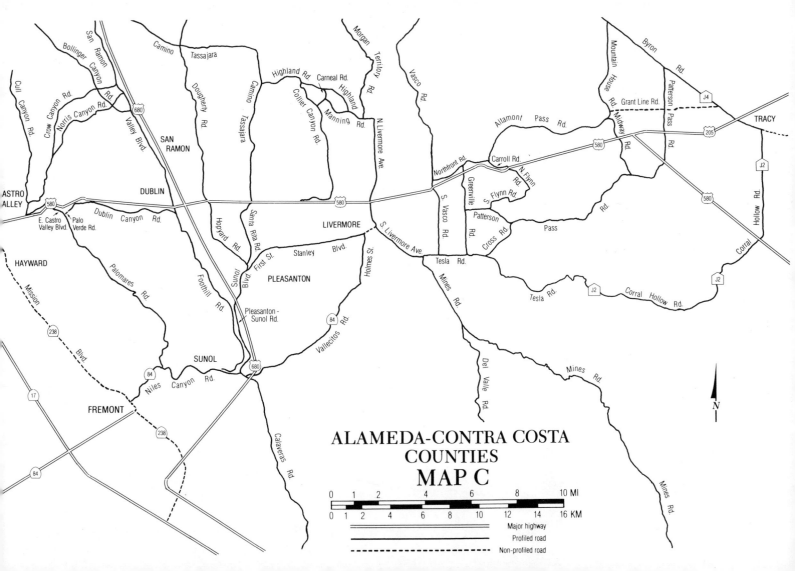

# ALAMEDA-CONTRA COSTA COUNTIES
## MAP C

| 0 | 1 | 2 | 4 | 6 | 8 | 10 MI |
|---|---|---|---|---|---|---|
| 0 | 1 | 2 | 4 | 6 | 8 | 10 | 12 | 14 | 16 KM |

———————— Major highway
———————— Profiled road
– – – – – – Non-profiled road

## Acalanes Rd. / Glorietta Blvd. (Map A)

A residential road that goes from Lafayette to Orinda. Of the reasonably direct routes between these two towns, this is the least hilly.

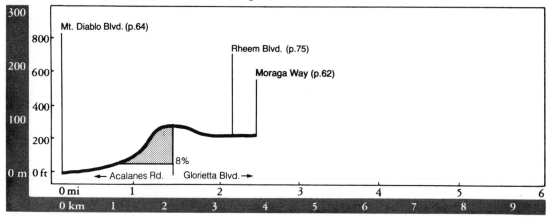

## Alhambra Valley Rd. (Map A)

A rural road that runs along the northern edge of the Briones-Bear Creek area. From Pinole Valley Rd. to Bear Creek Rd. it follows Pinole Creek through a wide valley. North of "Pig Farm Hill" the road levels out and travels through orchards and past ranch houses. Little shade and very little traffic.

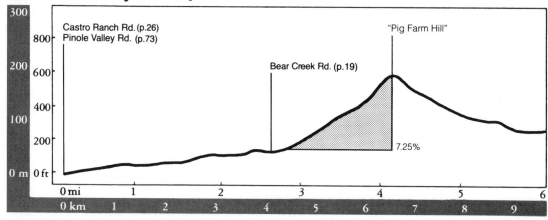

## Alhambra Valley Rd. *cont.*

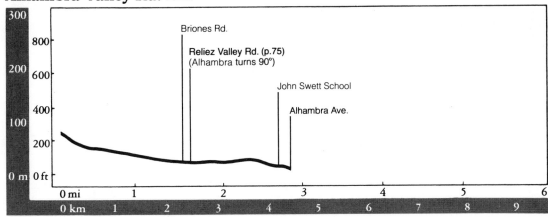

## Altamont Pass Rd. (Map C)

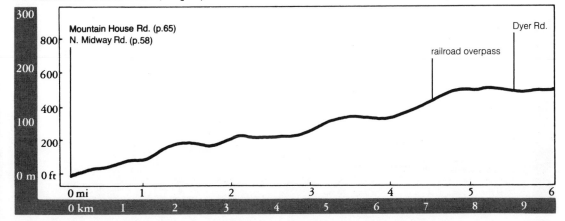

An enjoyable, though not striking road in the range land between Livermore and Tracy, in eastern Alameda County. It's usually quite windy, but there's very little traffic (except on weekends when there's often a lot of truck traffic on the road).

## Altamont Pass Rd. *cont.*

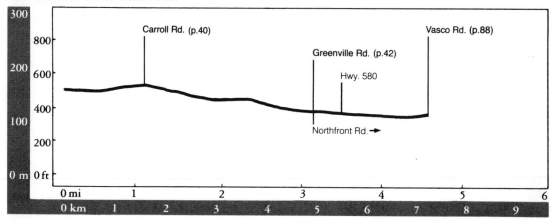

## Balfour Rd. (Map B)

A flat farm road with very little, and generally very local, traffic. It's near Brentwood.

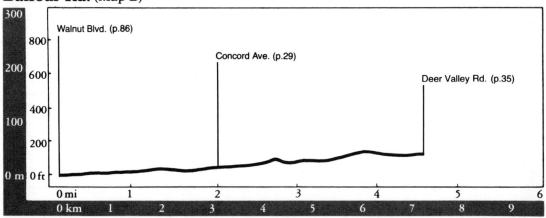

## Bear Creek Rd. (Map A)

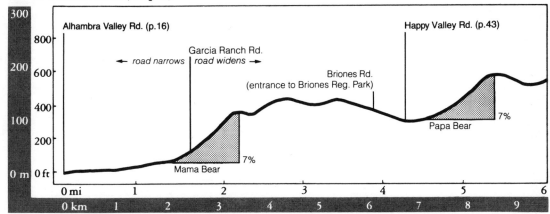

The northern mile and a half and the southernmost half mile of the road are narrow and wooded, with a few farmhouses along the way. The portion between is relatively open and unshaded, as it rolls along the pastures overlooking Briones Reservoir. Good surface, little traffic, laborious climbs, fast descents, and no turns that require braking.

## Bear Creek Rd. *cont.*

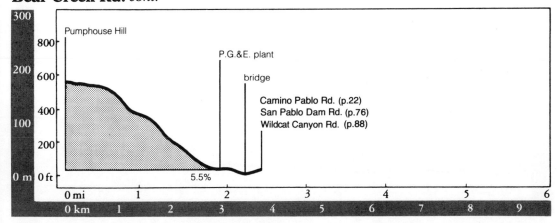

The portion of this road between San Ramon Valley Blvd. and Crow Canyon Rd. is relatively wide, smooth, and developed. North of Crow Canyon Rd. the road becomes much more rural and narrow, with an abrasive surface. The northern portion parallels Bollinger Canyon Creek, and the road ends as a picnic area on the edge of Las Trampas Regional Wilderness.

## Bollinger Canyon Rd. (Maps B,C)

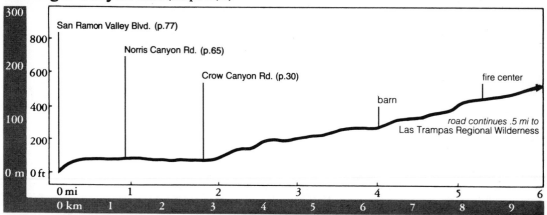

This road connects Sunol and Milpitas. The portion shown is extremely curvy, wooded and narrow with almost no traffic. The road continues to the south, keeping the same character. Enjoyable riding.

## Calaveras Rd. (Map C)

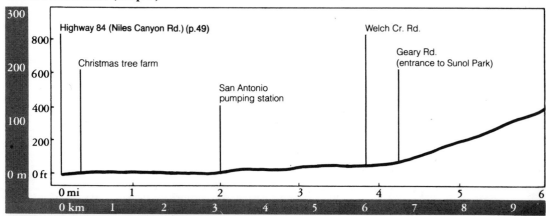

## Calaveras Rd. *cont.*

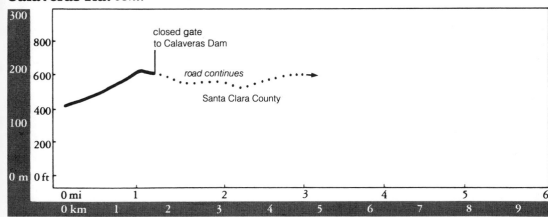

## Camino Diablo Rd. (Map B)

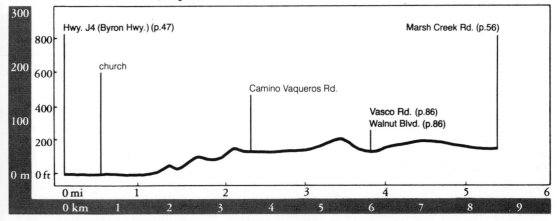

A lightly trafficked road in the
farmland west of Byron. The
surface is hard and gravelly.

## Camino Pablo (Map A)

A narrow, gently winding, residential road with lots of traffic. A bicycle/running path parallels it for much of its length on its east side.

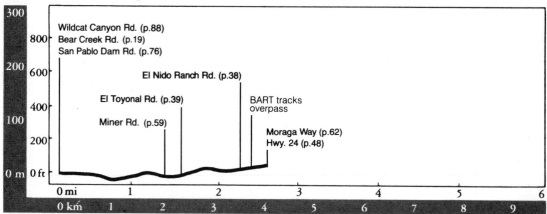

## Camino Tassajara (Maps B,C)

From Diablo Rd. in Danville, this road travels more or less east across rolling pastureland. At Finley Rd. it heads south and, continuing through the countryside, eventually meets Hwy 580 at Santa Rita Rd. The riding is excellent, the traffic is light, and the afternoon winds blow from the northwest.

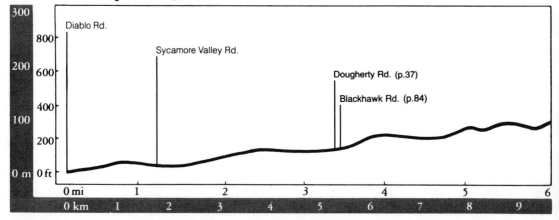

## Camino Tassajara *cont.*

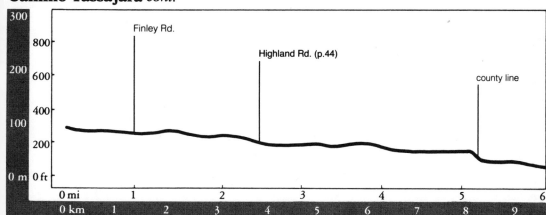

Finley Rd.

Highland Rd. (p.44)

county line

## Camino Tassajara *cont.*

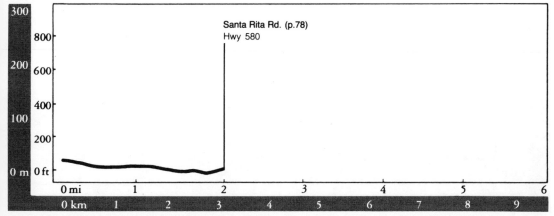

Santa Rita Rd. (p.78)
Hwy 580

## Canyon Rd. (Map A)

This road runs between Moraga Way and Pinehurst Rd. It's residential from Moraga Way, in downtown Moraga, to the bridge. Between the bridge and Pinehurst Rd., it's rolling, narrow, and wooded.

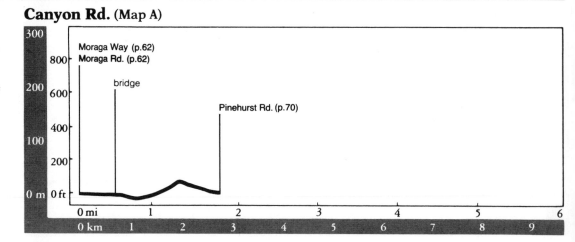

## Carneal Rd. (Maps B,C)

A short, fine road in the grazing land southeast of Danville. Since it is so short, it's not likely to be the main feature of any day's ride, but if you like riding a bicycle at all, you'll like Carneal Rd.

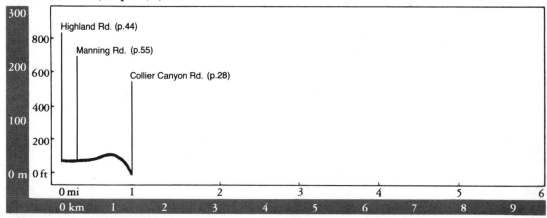

## Carquinez Scenic Dr. (Map A)

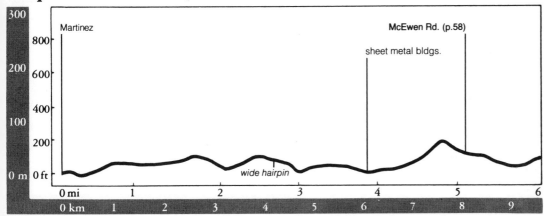

To get to this road from central Martinez, turn left on Escobar St., then right on Talbot St. Carquinez Scenic Dr. is a narrow, twisty road with no major climbs or descents, but plenty of minor ones. It's wooded, and travels along the hills overlooking the southern edge of the Carquinez Straits and many refineries.

## Carquinez Scenic Dr. *cont.*

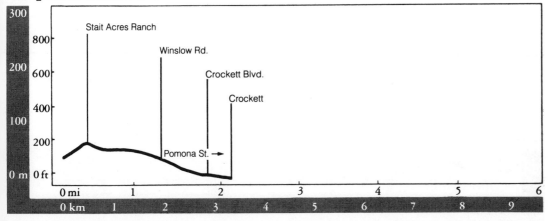

## Castle Crest Rd. (Map B)

Castle Crest was known as "The Hill" in the pre-bike boom years, because it was the steepest climb in the area. The appellation has been forgotten, but The Hill hasn't changed at all. The roads are residential and accessible from the north via Tice Valley Blvd., or from the east via Danville Blvd.

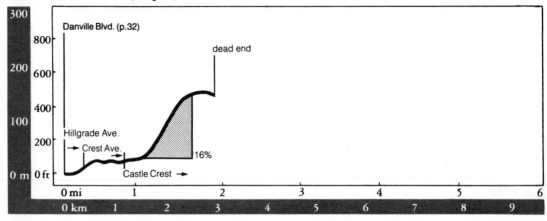

## Castro Ranch Rd. (Map A)

The western portion of this road, where it intersects San Pablo Dam Rd. just south of El Sobrante, is wide, smooth, and residential. The remainder is more rural, wooded, winding, and narrow.

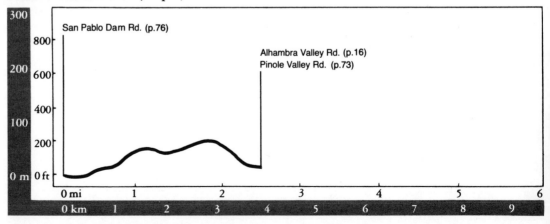

## Centennial Dr. (Map A)

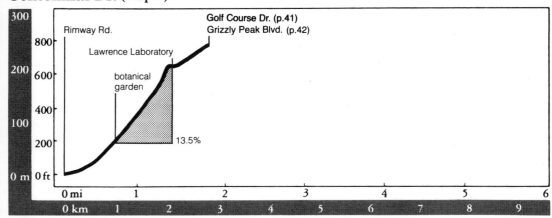

A steep and narrow road that winds up a relatively undeveloped portion (no residences or businesses) of the Berkeley hills. Most of the road is without shade, and it has a fair amount of traffic in the lower 1.5 miles. There are a couple of fields, a pool, and some UC-owned buildings on Centennial Dr., but what you'll notice mostly is the steepness. A direct route between the outskirts of the UC campus area and Grizzly Peak Blvd.

## Claremont Ave. (Map A)

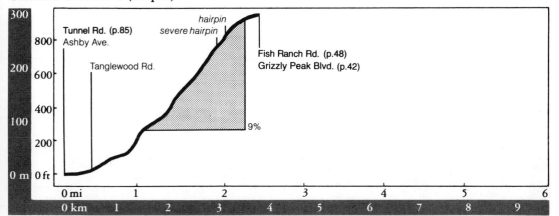

Somewhat residential at the bottom, steep and snaky near the top. One rather hairy hairpin turn near the top is the most difficult part of the climb, the most dangerous part of the descent. This profile begins at Ashby Ave., near the Claremont Hotel.

## Collier Canyon Rd. (Map C)

A narrow road with a rough
surface and a crumbly shoulder.
It travels through pastures
north of Livermore and Hwy 580.
For the first couple of miles it
parallels the freeway.

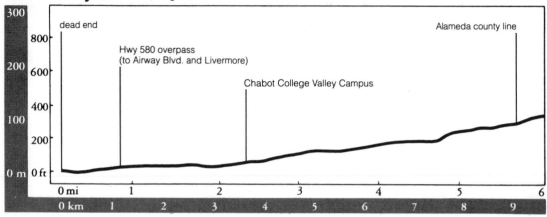

## Collier Canyon Rd. *cont.*

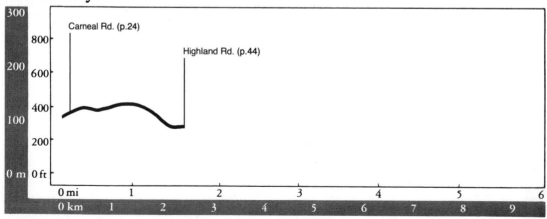

## Concord Ave. (Map B)

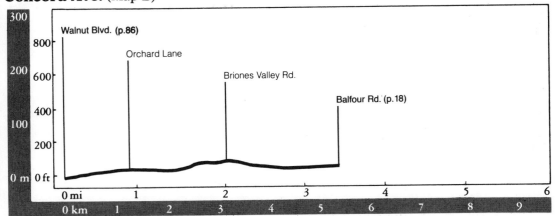

A rural road that takes you through pastures, orchards, and vineyards. It's quiet, has very little traffic, and is near Brentwood, not Concord.

## Cross Rd. (Map C)

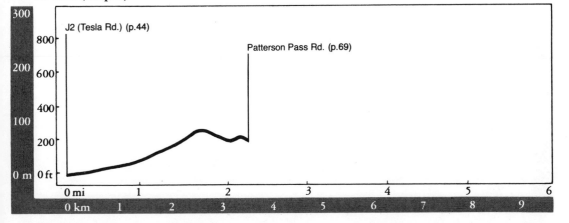

A short, little-known, and particularly fun road. Most riders are in this eastern Alameda County area to ride Patterson Pass Rd., Mines Rd., or some other prominent road. Relatively short roads like Cross Rd. (and Flynn Rd.) tend to get overlooked. Narrow, with no traffic.

A rolling, wooded thoroughfare between Castro Valley and the Danville-San Ramon area. Heavily trafficked during commute hours, but not bad at other times.

## Crow Canyon Rd. (Map C)

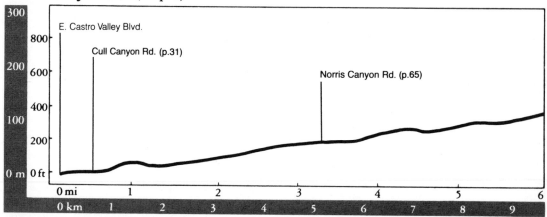

## Crow Canyon Rd. *cont.*

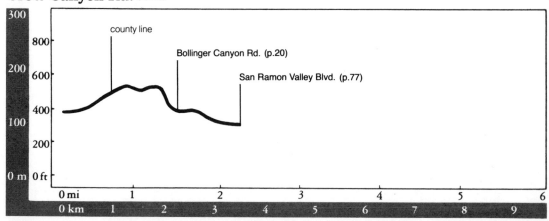

## Cull Canyon Rd. (Map C)

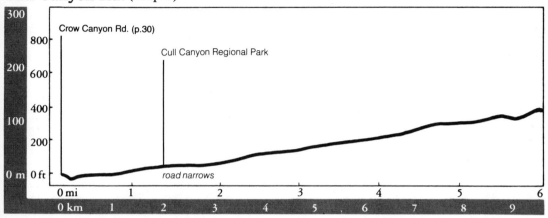

A dead end road just east of Castro Valley. It is wooded and narrow with lots of potholes, but very little traffic. The gradual uphill is long enough to provide a good workout, and the descent is fun and fast.

## Cull Canyon Rd. *cont.*

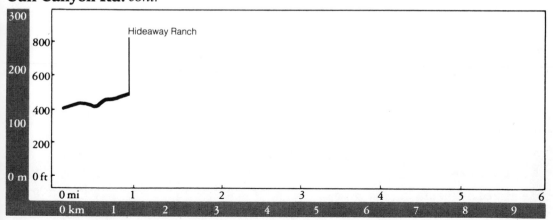

A fairly wide road in the pastures south of Crockett. Since it links Hwy 80 to Hwy 4, it has steady traffic. Most bicyclists will only ride the upper 2 miles between Crockett Blvd. and Franklin Canyon Rd.

## Cummings Skyway (Map A)

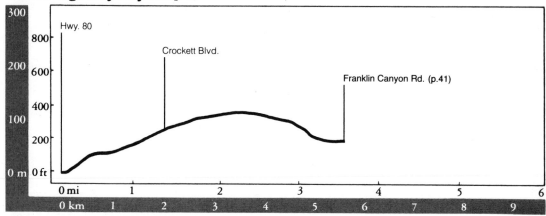

This road begins at South Main St. in Walnut Creek. It's a wide, residential road which parallels Hwy 680. There's a bike lane in both directions, and lots of car, bicycle, and runner traffic.

## Danville Blvd. (Map B)

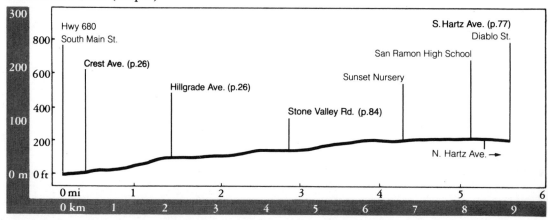

ONE
LANE
ROAD

NEXT
10 MILES

Mines Rd.

Cross Rd.

## Deer Valley Rd. (Map B)

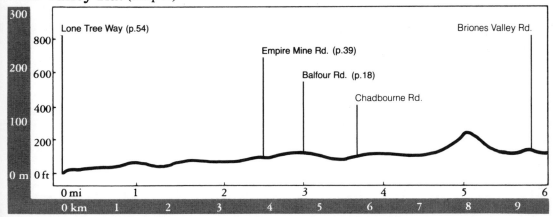

An eastern Contra Costa County farmland road. It's narrow with very little traffic and good riding.

## Deer Valley Rd. *cont.*

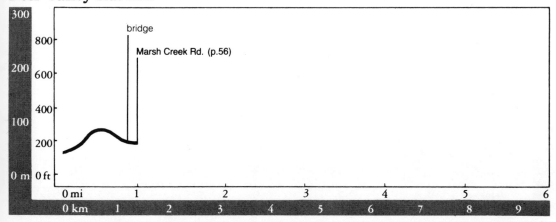

## Del Valle Rd. (Map C)

A wide, shadeless road with a good surface. It ends at the entrance to Lake Del Valle, a popular swimming and picnic area.

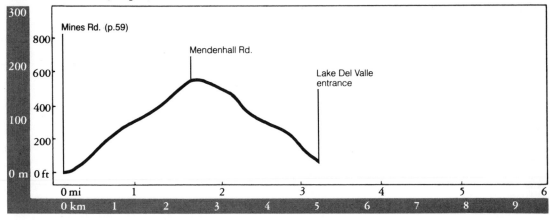

## Donald Dr./Hall Dr. (Map A)

An extremely difficult climb with a 360° view of the East Bay hills from the top. Both ends of the ride are wide, smooth, and residential. The upper portion, particularly on the Moraga Way (west) side, is narrow, uninhabited, and has a bumpy and broken surface.

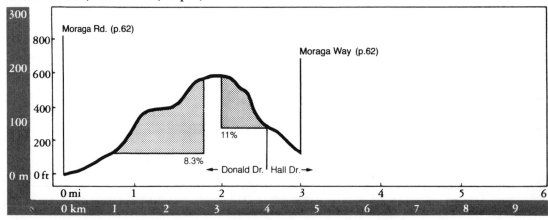

## Dougherty Rd. (Map C)

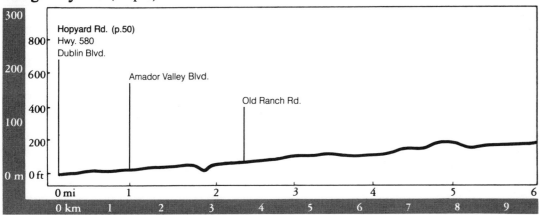

This is one of my favorite roads. It travels through rolling grazing land east of Danville and Dublin. Some of the worst potholes have recently been repaired, but the surface is still rather rough. Almost no traffic.

## Dougherty Rd. *cont.*

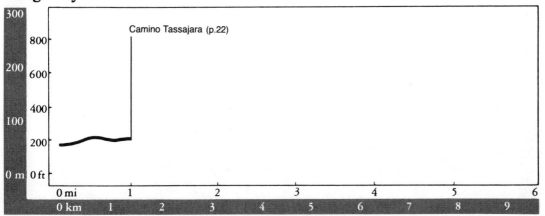

## Dublin Canyon Rd. (Map C)

This road roughly parallels Hwy 580 between Dublin and Castro Valley. It's a wide, smooth, freeway alternative with steady, high-speed traffic. There's a bike lane in the eastward direction. The western end connects to Palomares Rd. via Palo Verde Rd.

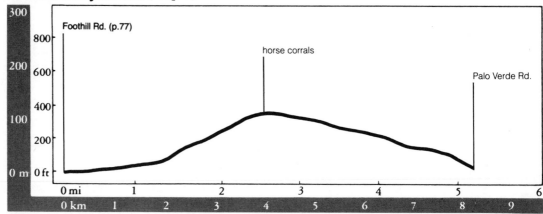

## El Nido Ranch Rd. (Map A)

A hilly, residential group of roads that roughly parallel Hwy 24 between Lafayette and Orinda. The climb out of Orinda past John F. Kennedy University is one of the most detestable short climbs around: very steep, out in the sun, and not particularly pretty.

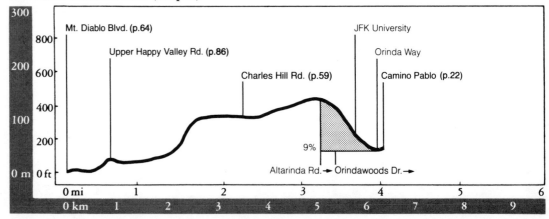

## El Toyonal Rd. (Map A)

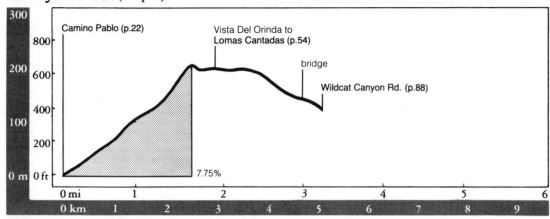

An enjoyable road between Camino Pablo Rd. in Orinda, and Wildcat Canyon Rd. It's steep, narrow, and densely wooded except for the steepest part which is residential. El Toyonal is particularly useful as a good workout and as an alternative access to the Berkeley hills. Note: the flood of '83 washed out a section of this road. Until it's repaired, walk your bike through this part.

## Empire Mine Rd. (Map B)

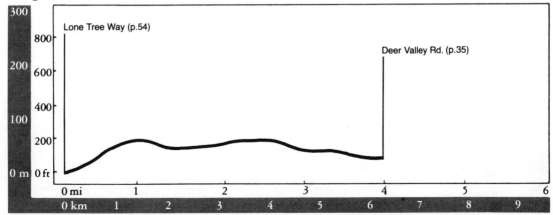

An often neglected farm road in northeastern Contra Costa County. It's narrow with a gravelly surface and sloping shoulders. There's almost no traffic.

## First St./Stanley Blvd. (Map C)

First St. is a main thoroughfare through downtown Pleasanton, and typical of such streets in small-town business districts. It becomes Stanley Blvd. where it curves eastward, and from there it's straight all the way to Livermore. It parallels railroad tracks on one side and a bicycle/footpath on the other. There's a steady flow of traffic, but sufficient room to ride. This road is strictly utilitarian and rather boring.

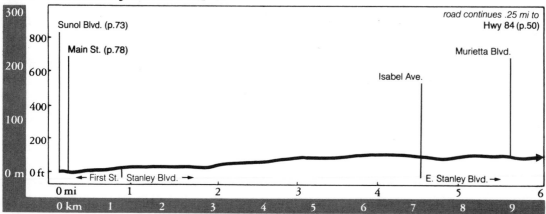

## Flynn Rds./Carroll Rd. (Map C)

North Flynn Rd. and South Flynn Rd. are hilly, quite narrow, deserted, and perfectly good riding roads. Carroll Rd. is similar but a bit wider. As a group, they connect Patterson Pass Rd. (near the Lawrence Livermore Lab) with Altamont Pass Rd.

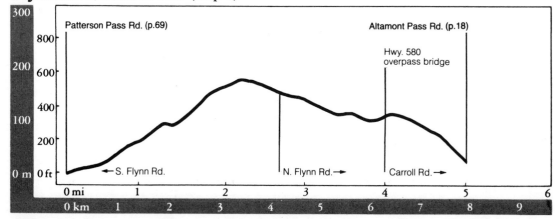

## Franklin Canyon Rd. (Map A)

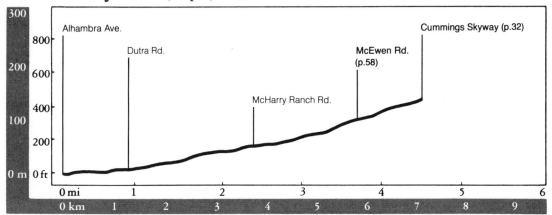

Beginning at Alhambra Ave. below the Hwy 4 overpass, Franklin Canyon Rd. winds gently up the canyon as a narrow, wooded road with a few houses. It opens up a bit before it connects with Cummings Skyway.

## Golf Course Dr. (Map A)

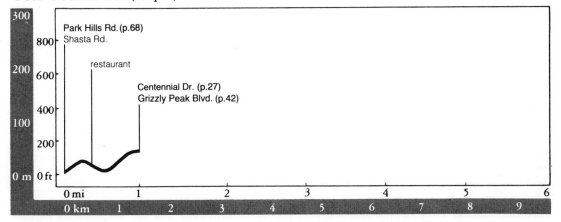

Golf Course Dr. begins at the junction of Shasta Rd. and Park Hills Rd. in Tilden Park above Lake Anza. There's a kiosk there. It's a rough-surfaced, narrow road, and it passes Tilden's golf course. It connects to Grizzly Peak Blvd. at Centennial Dr.

## Greenville Rd. (Map C)

A straight and narrow rural road that travels north-south between Altamont Pass Rd. and Tesla Rd. (J2). It borders the east side of the Lawrence Livermore Lab.

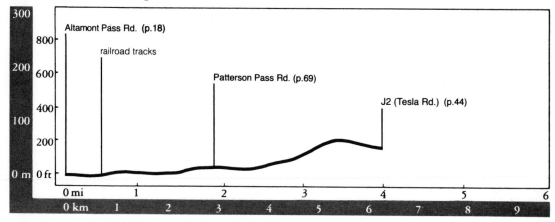

## Grizzly Peak Blvd. (Map A)

The longest, highest road in the Berkeley hills. The lower couple of miles, from Spruce St. to Centennial Dr. are residential, but the rest of it curves and rolls (mostly gently) along the crest of the hills. The riding is fun and the views are good. Traffic is heavier on weekends, but never too bad.

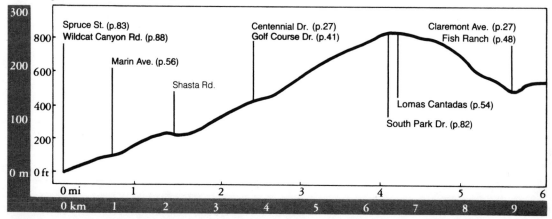

## Grizzly Peak Blvd. *cont.*

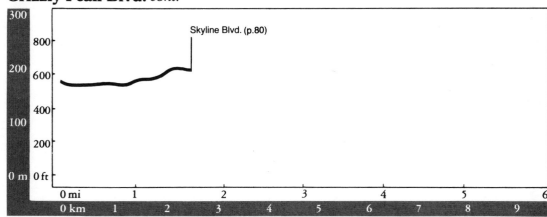

Skyline Blvd. (p.80)

## Happy Valley Rd. (Map A)

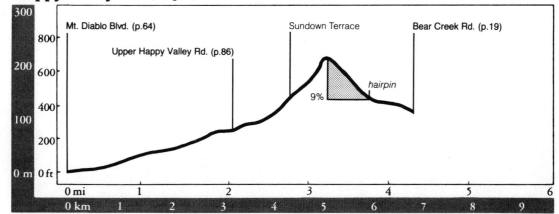

Mt. Diablo Blvd. (p.64)

Upper Happy Valley Rd. (p.86)

Sundown Terrace

Bear Creek Rd. (p.19)

9%

*hairpin*

A wooded, straight, narrow residential road for the lower couple of miles. The hill is steep and winding.

## Highland Rd. (Maps B,C)

A quiet country road in the southern foothills of Mt. Diablo. It's pretty in the winter and early spring—all green and bright yellow. A nice road.

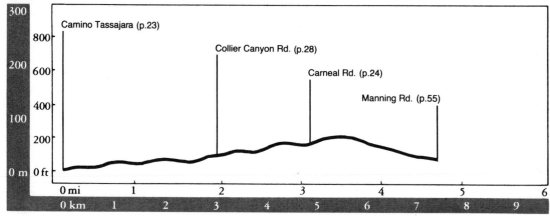

Camino Tassajara (p.23)

Collier Canyon Rd. (p.28)

Carneal Rd. (p.24)

Manning Rd. (p.55)

## Highway J2 (Tesla Rd., etc.) (Map C)

This begins as South Livermore Ave. in downtown Livermore. After a couple of miles of mixed city and residential riding, it heads east as Tesla Rd., through farmland and vineyards, for several miles. As it climbs, the scenery changes to large treeless hills. There's a good view to the east from the summit. The east side is rugged and pretty; descending it is a lot of fun. Between Carnegie Recreation Area and J4 it's a lot less spectacular.

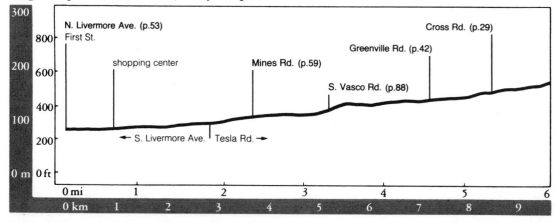

N. Livermore Ave. (p.53)
First St.

Cross Rd. (p.29)

shopping center

Greenville Rd. (p.42)

Mines Rd. (p.59)

S. Vasco Rd. (p.88)

← S. Livermore Ave. | Tesla Rd. →

## Highway J2 *cont.*

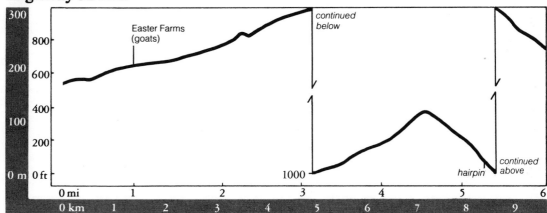

## Highway J2 *cont.*

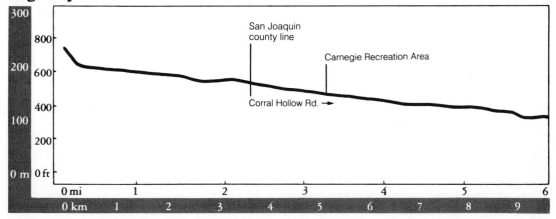

## Highway J2 *cont.*

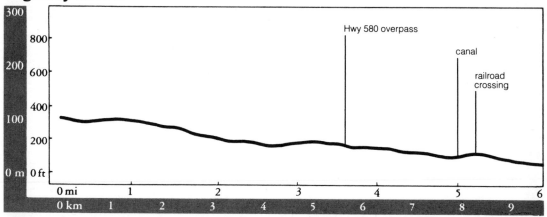

## Highway J2 *cont.*

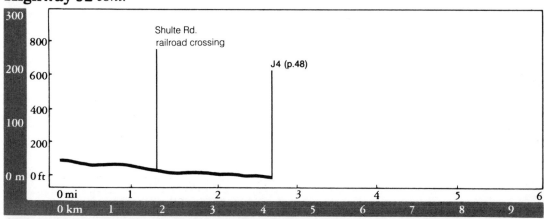

## Highway J4 (Maps B,C)

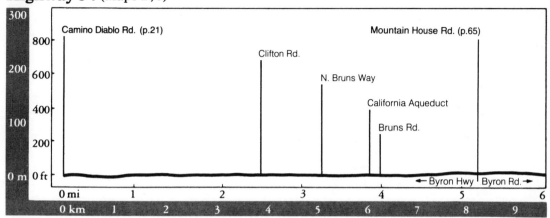

This runs between Byron and Tracy, on the eastern edge of Contra Costa County. It's a flat road with a lot of wind and traffic—including large trucks. It goes through farmland and seems endless.

## Highway J4 *cont.*

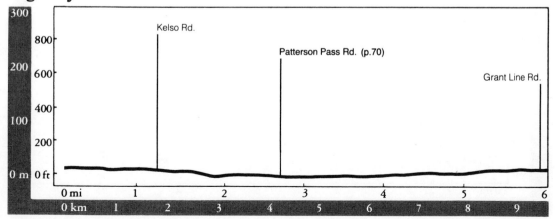

## Highway J4 *cont.*

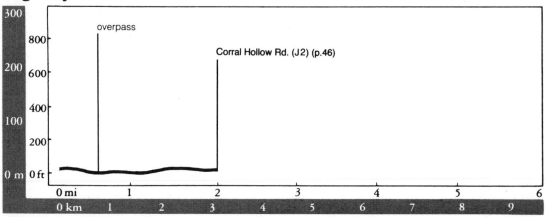

Highway J4 continued: elevation profile showing "overpass" at about 0.5 mi and "Corral Hollow Rd. (J2) (p.46)" at about 2 mi. Elevation scale in feet (0, 200, 400, 600, 800) and meters (0 m, 100, 200, 300); distance scale 0–6 mi and 0–9 km.

## Highway 24/Fish Ranch Rd. (Map A)

Hwy 24 is bicycle-legal between Orinda and Fish Ranch Rd. (You must exit at Gateway Blvd., but you can get right back on.) It's no fun, but there's plenty of room and it's faster than taking Pinehurst Rd. or Wildcat Canyon Rd. if you're riding to Berkeley from Orinda. Fish Ranch Rd. is fine—not much traffic, wooded, and rather pretty.

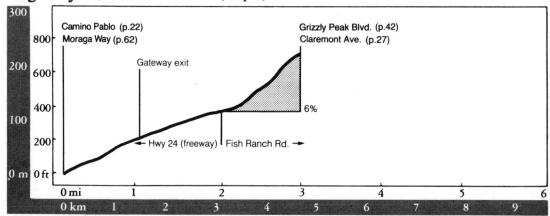

Highway 24/Fish Ranch Rd. elevation profile. Labels: "Camino Pablo (p.22)", "Moraga Way (p.62)" at start; "Grizzly Peak Blvd. (p.42)", "Claremont Ave. (p.27)" at end; "Gateway exit" at about 1.1 mi; "Hwy 24 (freeway)" and "Fish Ranch Rd." along lower portion; "6%" grade marked near the climb. Elevation scale 0 ft–800 ft and 0 m–300 m; distance 0–6 mi and 0–9 km.

## Highway 84 (Niles Canyon Rd., etc.) (Map C)

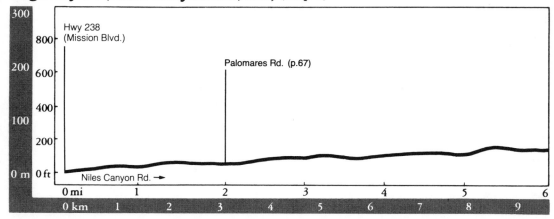

The western portion of Hwy 84 is a wooded, curvy road that follows a creek through a deep canyon (Niles Canyon). There are a lot of picnic areas and public-access fishing and swimming spots along this portion, and the weekend traffic can be thick. Between Hwy 680 and the point at which it becomes Holmes St., it travels over fairly unspectacular hills. There's less traffic on this portion, and the road is much straighter. The couple of miles

## Highway 84 *cont.*

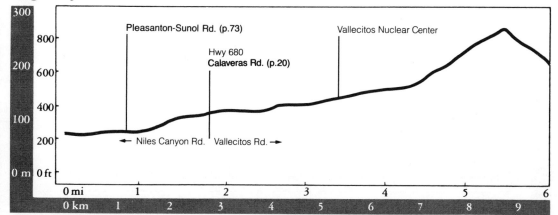

nearest to downtown Livermore are wide, busy, and urban.

## Highway 84 *cont.*

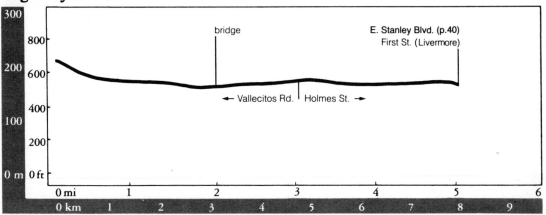

## Hopyard Rd. (Map C)

A flat, extremely busy urban road. Its only use for cyclists is as a route between the southern end of Dougherty Rd. and downtown Pleasanton.

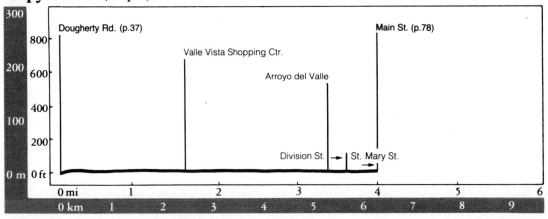

Corral Hollow Rd.

Dougherty Rd.

## Joaquin Miller Rd. (Map A)

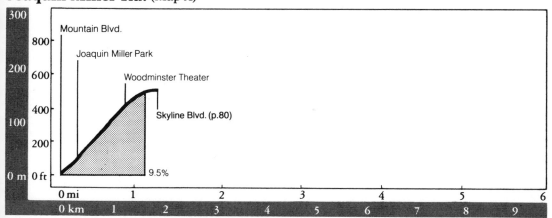

Joaquin Miller Rd. is a four-lane divided road, which is really neither pretty nor ugly. It's wide, has a good surface, a few minor intersections, and a lot of parked cars.

## Livermore Ave., North (Maps C)

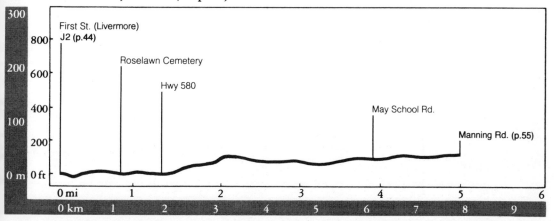

This road begins at First St. in Livermore (by the fountain). The first 1.5 miles are busy and urban. Between Hwy 580 and the 90° corner where it meets Manning Rd., North Livermore Ave. is a straight and narrow road through grazing land. The wind usually blows from the north.

## Lomas Cantadas (Map A)

This is the steepest road into the Berkeley hills from the east side. You can reach its bottom, a short road called Vista del Orinda, via El Toyonal (see page 39). After climbing Vista del Orinda for anywhere from 25 seconds to a minute and a half, turn south on Las Piedras, which joins Lomas Cantadas in a short distance. The road is wooded, winding, mostly residential, and has an overall average grade of 10.25%.

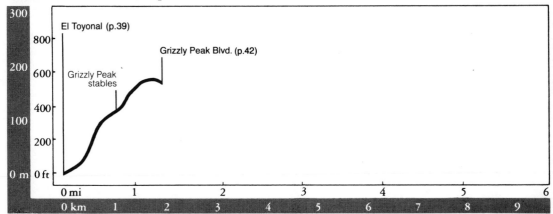

## Lone Tree Way (Map B)

This road's northern end is just south of downtown Antioch. The road's character and riding change near the golf course, and it becomes a flat, country road bordered on both sides by pastures and grazing cattle. Narrow, with little traffic.

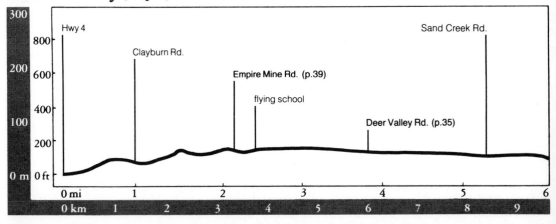

## Lone Tree Way *cont.*

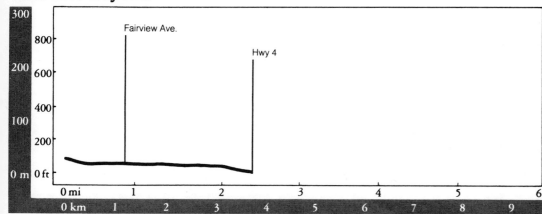

Fairview Ave.

Hwy 4

## Manning Rd. (Maps B,C)

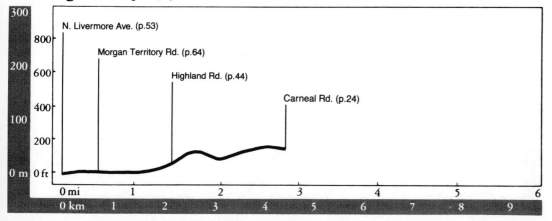

N. Livermore Ave. (p.53)

Morgan Territory Rd. (p.64)

Highland Rd. (p.44)

Carneal Rd. (p.24)

This road is typical of other roads in the pasturelands between Mt. Diablo and Livermore: narrow, almost no traffic, and enjoyable to ride. The eastern end of Manning Rd. and the northern end of North Livermore Ave. form a sharp corner about a half mile east of Morgan Territory Rd.

## Marin Ave. (Map A)

The steepest route into the Berkeley hills from the west side. This is a completely residential road. It almost levels out at each cross street. I can run up this road faster than I can ride up it, and that's probably true for most people.

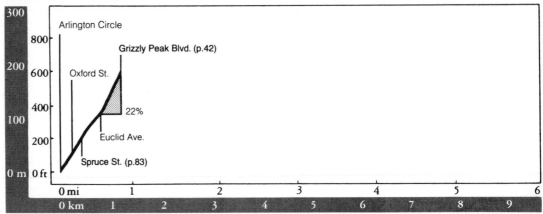

## Marsh Creek Rd. (Map B)

A narrow, wooded, bumpy road that borders Mt. Diablo. A good road for fit bicyclists, it is usually part of a long ride.

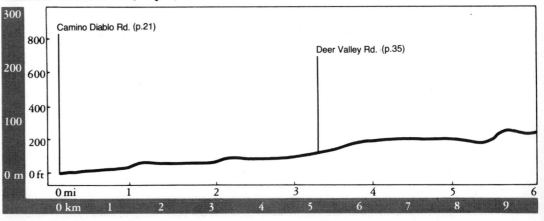

## Marsh Creek Rd. *cont.*

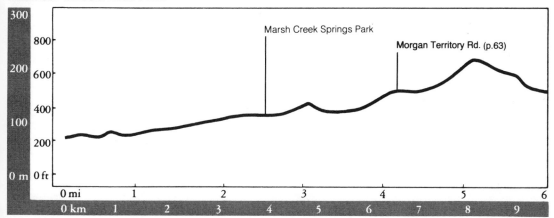

## Marsh Creek Rd. *cont.*

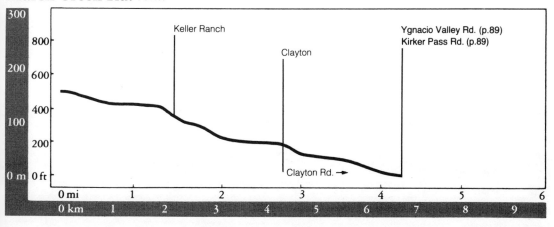

## McEwen Rd. (Map A)

A narrow, winding road over the rolling hills near Crockett. The steep portion parallels a tiny canyon that's rather pretty. There's very little traffic. An especially fun road.

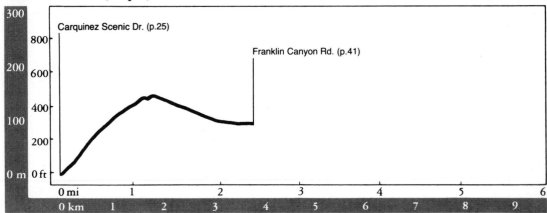

## Midway Rd. (Maps C)

A short connector road in the range land between Patterson Pass Rd. and Altamont Pass Rd., east of Livermore. If you are coming from Livermore and are riding the Patterson Pass/Altamont loop, using Midway Rd. gets you out of riding the least desirable portion of Patterson Pass Rd.

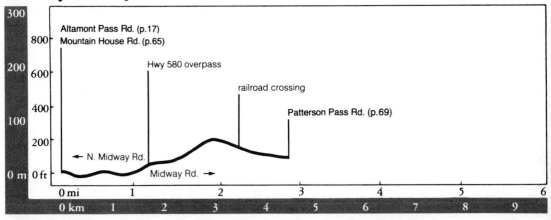

## Miner Rd. (Map A)

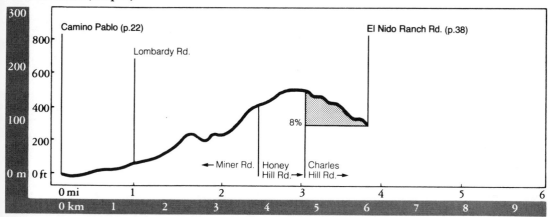

One of several indirect routes between Orinda and Lafayette, this one is residential, wooded, and challenging. Coming from Orinda, don't miss the turn onto Honey Hill Rd. just before a steep descent. Coming from Lafayette, continue straight up the incline onto Honey Hill Rd. beyond the point at which Charles Hill Rd. curves sharply to the right. The lower mile and a half has steady traffic during commute hours.

## Mines Rd. (Map C)

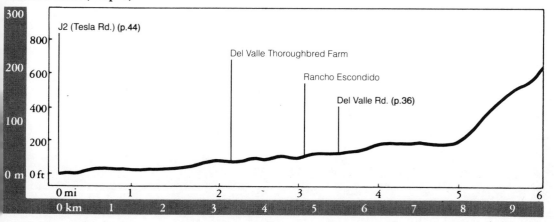

This road turns south from J2 a few miles out of Livermore. After a few flat miles among farms and vineyards it leaves all signs of civilization behind, and you'll feel conspicuous riding a bicycle—a horse would fit in with the deep, rugged canyon a lot better. Excellent riding on a narrow road with very little traffic. I once rode for an hour and a half on this road without seeing a car.

## **Mines Rd.** *cont.*

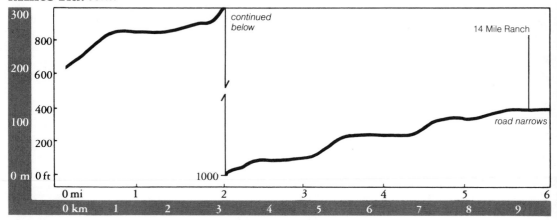

## **Mines Rd.** *cont.*

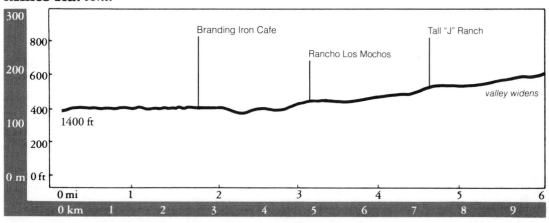

# Mines Rd. *cont.*

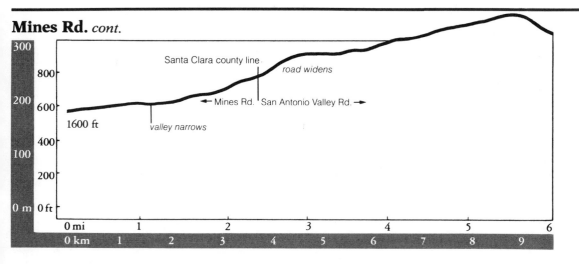

# Mines Rd. *cont.*

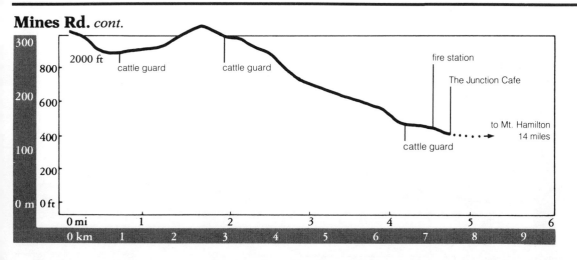

The main road between downtown Lafayette and Moraga.
The fairly steep 1.5 mile climb
is narrow, winding, and mostly
wooded. The rest of Moraga Rd.
is a normal, four-lane urban
business road.

## Moraga Rd. (Map A)

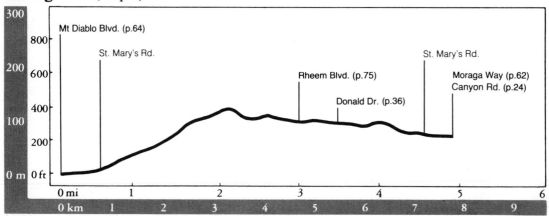

The main road between downtown Orinda and Moraga. Tree-
lined, narrow, fairly straight,
and residential, with quite a
lot of traffic. More useful than
fun.

## Moraga Way (Map A)

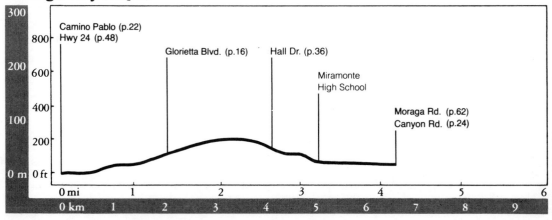

## Morgan Territory Rd. (Map C)

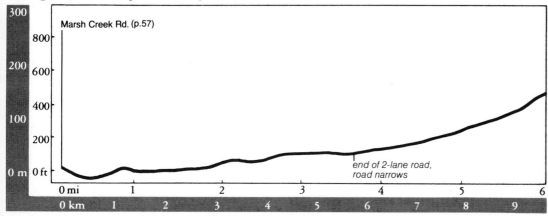

*Marsh Creek Rd. (p.57)*

end of 2-lane road, road narrows

On the east side of Mt. Diablo between Marsh Creek Rd. and Manning Rd. The southern side, towards Highland and Manning Rds., is extremely narrow and curvy, with an average grade of 7.5%. It travels through shadeless range country. The northern side is wooded, shady, while continuing narrow and winding. Almost no traffic. A fun road. The average grade of the entire road is 5.4%.

## Morgan Territory Rd. *cont.*

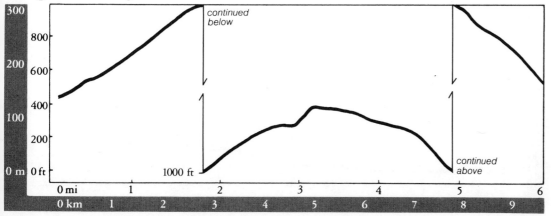

*continued below*

1000 ft

*continued above*

## Morgan Territory Rd. *cont.*

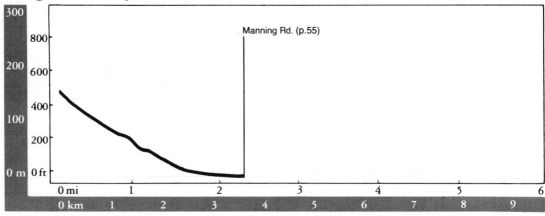

## Mount Diablo Blvd. (Map A)

Downtown Lafayette's main street, complete with gas stations, grocery stores, and fast food joints. The western end of it (near the Lafayette Reservoir) is not developed.

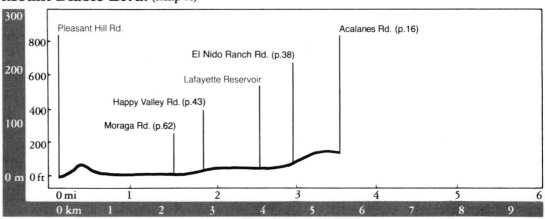

## Mountain House Rd. (Maps B,C)

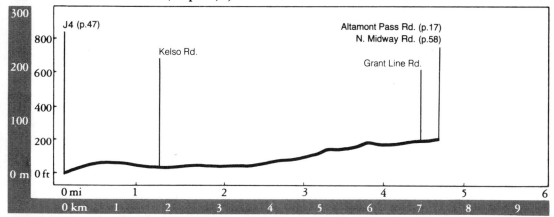

A rural road in eastern Alameda County between the Byron Hwy (J4) and Altamont Pass Rd. Lightly travelled, with occasional strong winds.

## Norris Canyon Rd. (Maps B,C)

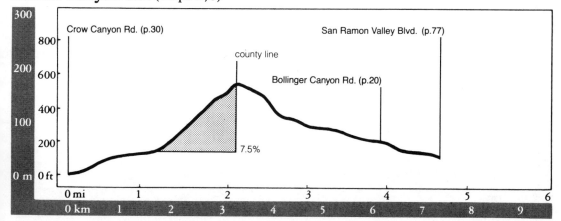

A wooded, hilly road with relatively little traffic. It has less car traffic than Crow Canyon Rd., and is close enough to it to be a reasonable alternative.

This road begins at the junction of Walnut Ave. and Oak Grove Rd. in eastern Walnut Creek and climbs towards the summit of Mt. Diablo. The last 6.5 mile stretch is a continuous tough climb with an average grade of 5.75%. Beautiful hills, with lots of lupines and poppies in the spring.

## North Gate Rd. (Map B)

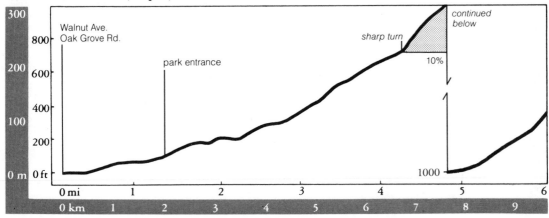

## North Gate Rd. *cont.*

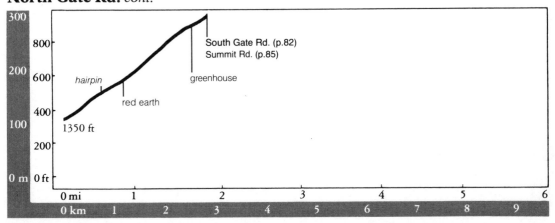

## Old San Pablo Dam Rd. (Map A)

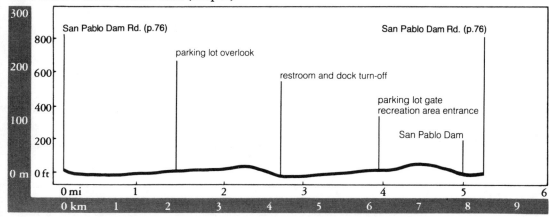

About a half mile north of where San Pablo Dam Rd., meets Wildcat Canyon and Bear Creek Rds., there's a dip down onto this, the original San Pablo Dam Rd. It follows the shoreline of San Pablo Reservoir, and most of it is unpaved. Balloon tires are well suited to this type of road, but you can manage on narrow tires if you don't mind walking a little. Don't wear cleats; eat lunch on the dam.

## Palomares Rd. (Map C)

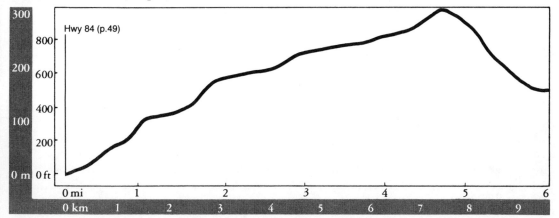

Palomares Rd. travels between Hwy 84 (Niles Canyon Rd.) and Dublin Canyon Rd., in the relatively untouched expanse between Fremont and Hayward (on the west) and Dublin and Pleasanton (on the east). It's a wooded, narrow road with an unkempt surface that snakes its way through the canyon between the Walpert (west) and Sunol (east) ridges. You get the feeling it hasn't changed in many years. It has an average grade of 4.25%.

## Palomares Rd. *cont.*

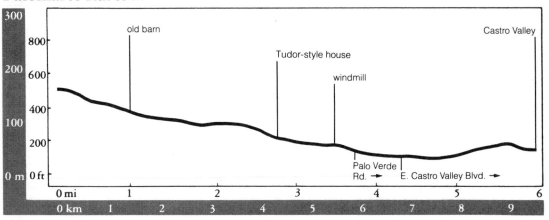

## Park Hills Rd. (Map A)

Park Hills Rd. is an extremely steep residential road in Tilden Park above Lake Anza. It's good exercise to ride short, very steep hills every now and then.

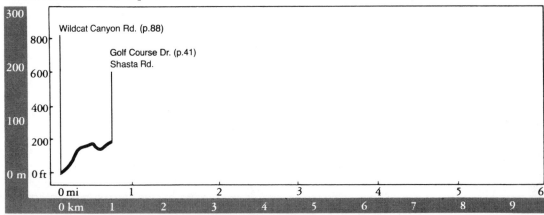

## Patterson Pass Rd. (Map C)

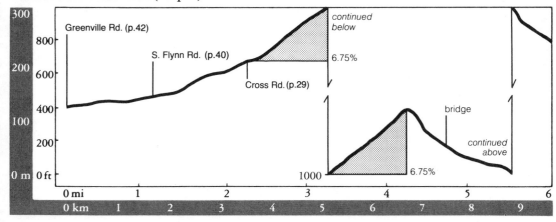

Greenville Rd. (p.42)

S. Flynn Rd. (p.40)

Cross Rd. (p.29)

continued below

6.75%

continued above

bridge

6.75%

A fun road for fit bicyclists, Patterson Pass Rd. is a little-travelled, narrow road between the Lawrence Livermore Lab and J4 (Byron Rd.). The four miles or so between Hwy 580 and J4 are kind of boring. When coming from Livermore, I prefer to turn north on Midway Rd., then west on Altamont Pass Rd., so I don't have to ride J4.

## Patterson Pass Rd. *cont.*

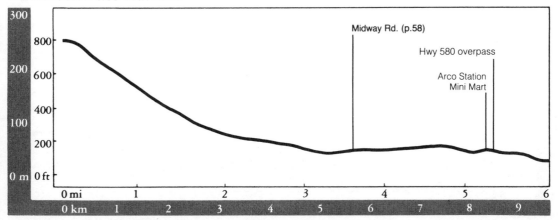

Midway Rd. (p.58)

Hwy 580 overpass

Arco Station
Mini Mart

## Patterson Pass Rd. *cont.*

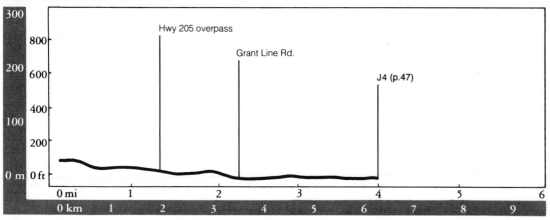

## Pinehurst Rd. (Map A)

Between Skyline Blvd. and Canyon Rd., Pinehurst Rd. is densely wooded and very narrow. The hill is curvy; the gradual portion, straight. Between Canyon Rd. (which leads to Moraga) and Redwood Rd., it's smoother with a lot less shade and more of a view. A very popular road. Not much traffic.

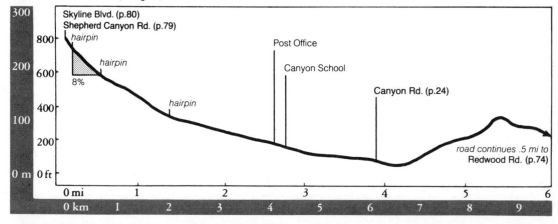

Palomares Rd.

Redwood Rd.

## Pinole Valley Rd. (Map A)

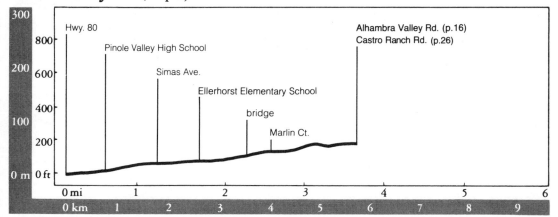

This road begins on the southern side of central Pinole, and most of it travels through a business district. The last mile or so has much less traffic, and becomes narrow and rural. Pinole Valley Rd. is primarily an access road to longer, more enjoyable roads.

## Pleasanton-Sunol Rd. (Map C)

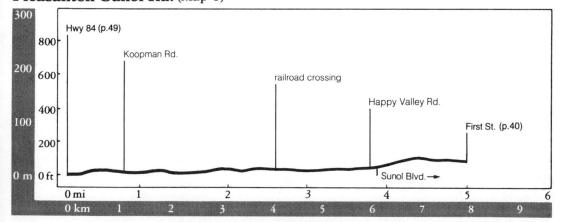

A narrow, wooded road that parallels Hwy 680 (but at a lower elevation) and runs more or less between Pleasanton and Sunol. It has an abrasive surface with a crumbly shoulder for much of its length, and light traffic.

35th Ave. in Oakland becomes Redwood Rd. east of Jordan St. The first mile or so is extremely busy, since it's on the outskirts of downtown Oakland. The steep climb is four lanes and divided. The rest of the road, from Skyline Blvd. to Castro Valley, is beautiful. It's narrow, winds its way through redwoods, and offers views of the surrounding hills.

## Redwood Rd. (Map A)

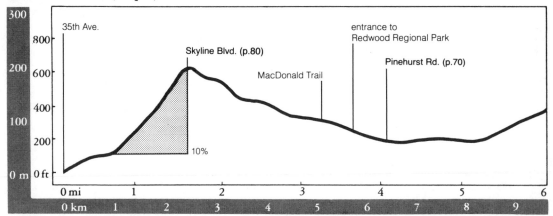

## Redwood Rd. *cont.*

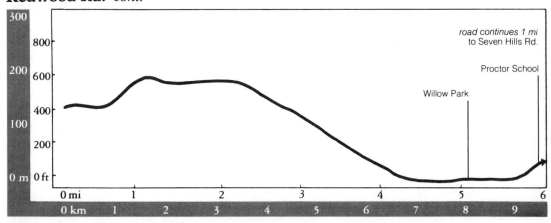

## Reliez Valley Rd. (Map A)

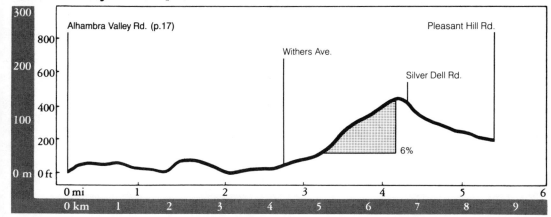

A wooded, narrow road between Alhambra Valley Rd. and Pleasant Hill Rd. northeast of Lafayette. The two miles or so closest to Pleasant Hill Rd. are residential, but most of it is rural.

## Rheem Blvd. (Map A)

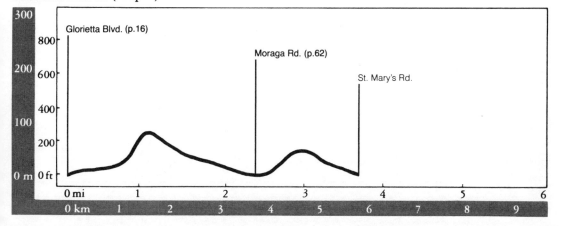

Rheem Blvd. is a hilly, mostly residential road between Glorietta Blvd. in Orinda and St. Mary's Rd. in Moraga. This is a useful road and doesn't have a lot of traffic, but it's not enough fun to be the highlight of a ride.

Between San Pablo Ave. and Tri Lane, this is a busy, residential and business road with many facilities but no particular appeal for bicyclists. The southern 5.5 miles between Tri Lane and Bear Creek Rd. pass through woodlands and border San Pablo Reservoir. This portion is rather wide and smooth, usually windy, and has a steady though not heavy flow of traffic.

## San Pablo Dam Rd. (Map A)

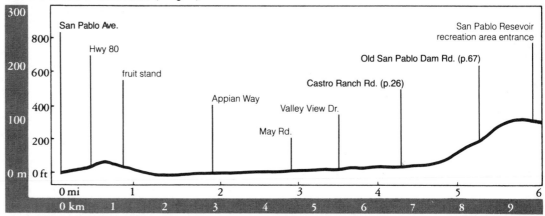

## San Pablo Dam Rd. *cont.*

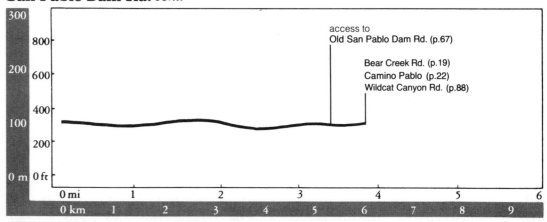

## San Ramon Valley Blvd./Foothill Rd. (Maps B,C)

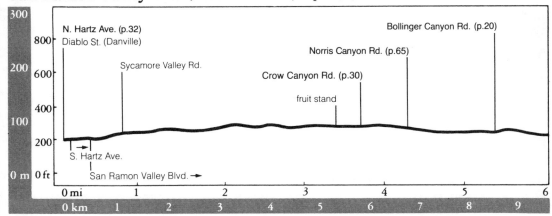

This is a southern extension of Danville Blvd. It parallels Hwy 680 between Danville and Sunol. Between Danville and Dublin it is lightly residential, has a steady though not particularly heavy flow of traffic, and has bike lanes. South of Dublin it is narrower, more rural, more enjoyable, and has less traffic. Riding northward in the afternoon, you're likely to hit headwinds.

## San Ramon Valley Blvd./Foothill Rd. *cont.*

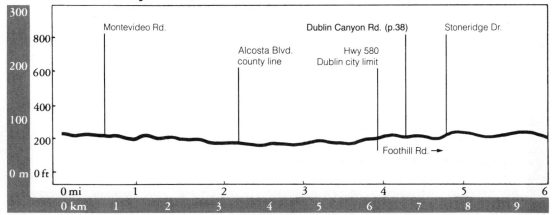

## San Ramon Valley Blvd./Foothill Rd. *cont.*

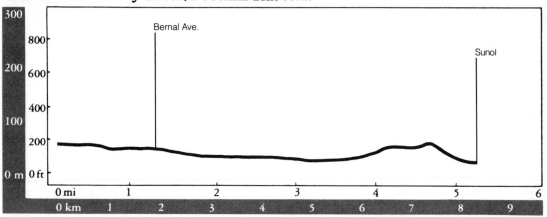

## Santa Rita Rd. (Map C)

This road connects the southern end of Camino Tassajara with downtown Pleasanton. It's busy, developed, and travels through residential and business areas.

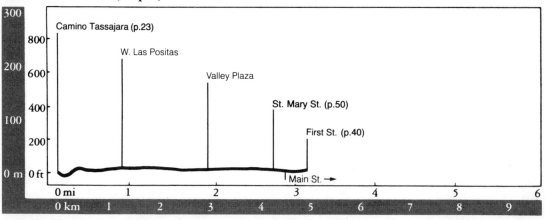

## Shepherd Canyon Rd. (Map A)

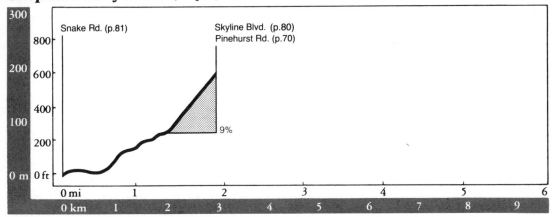

A way to get between the Montclair District in Oakland and Skyline Blvd. Snake Rd. is another alternative, but Shepherd Canyon Rd. has even less traffic. It meets Skyline Blvd. at nearly the same spot that Pinehurst Rd. does.

## Skyline Blvd. (Map A)

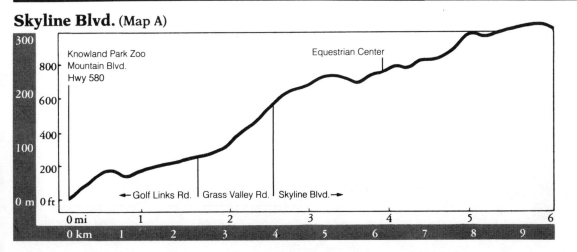

Typical of Skyline Boulevards wherever they exist, this one travels more or less on top of a range of hills, providing relatively high elevation riding and occasional distant views of the surrounding land. It's lightly residential, wooded, winding, and enjoyable. It passes several regional parks and preserves.

## Skyline Blvd. *cont.*

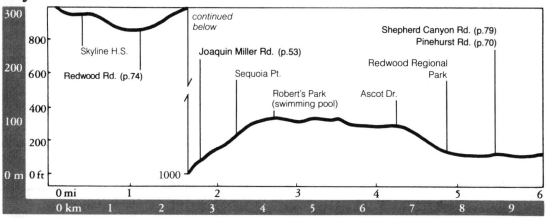

## Skyline Blvd. *cont.*

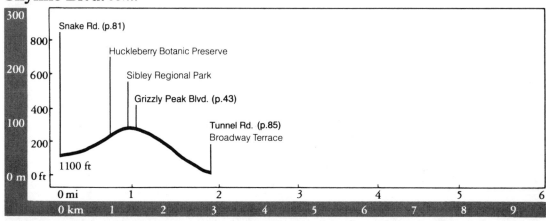

## Snake Rd. (Map A)

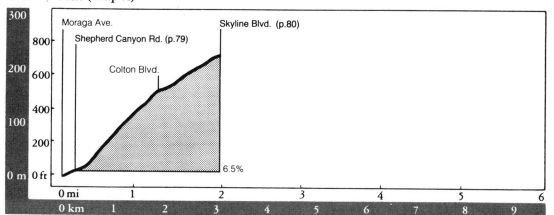

A steep, wooded, curvy, residential road from the Montclair District of Oakland to Skyline Blvd.

## South Gate Rd. (Map B)

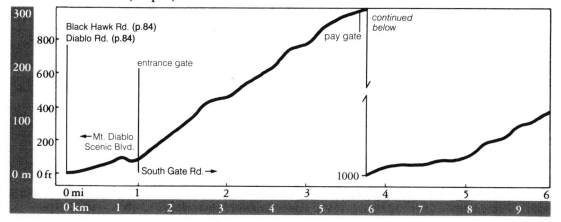

This road goes from Diablo Rd. east of Danville toward the summit of Mt. Diablo. It has an average grade of 4.5%. An easier, more enjoyable, more scenic road than North Gate Rd.

## South Gate Rd. *cont.*

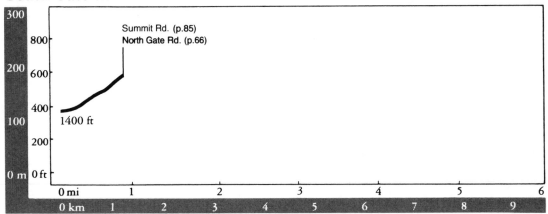

## South Park Dr. (Map A)

This road in the southern part of Tilden Park connects Wildcat Canyon Rd. (near the Tilden Botanical Garden) with Grizzly Peak Blvd. (near its highest point). It passes picnic areas, a trailhead, and a golf course, but you're either working too hard or descending too fast to really notice. South Park Dr. is probably the fastest descent in the Berkeley hills, due to both the steep grade and the lack of sharp curves. There's little traffic.

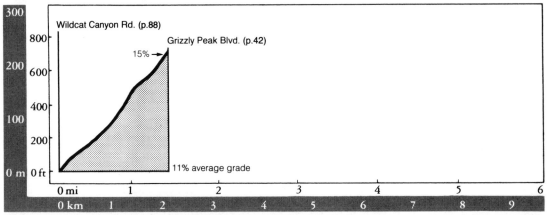

## Springhill Rd./Martino Rd. (Map A)

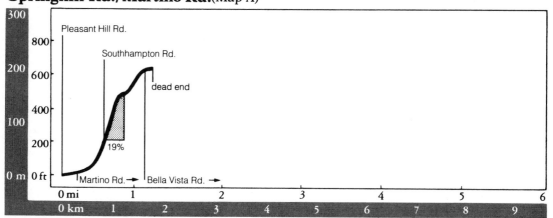

This is the steepest road that I know of in Contra Costa County. The view of Lafayette from the top is excellent, but it still may not be worth the effort. To reach it, take Springhill Rd. off Pleasant Hill Rd. Near the top, turn right on Bella Vista Rd. to the dead end.

## Spruce St. (Map A)

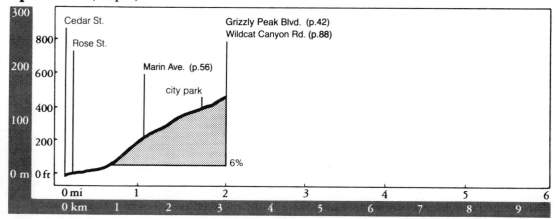

This busy residential street is the one that most riders use to get into and out of the Berkeley hills from the Berkeley side. Much of it is lined with parked cars, traffic is steady, there are many intersections, and the surface isn't very good. Useful, but not particularly fun.

A group of connecting roads that travel through both rural and residential areas between Alamo and the flats east of Danville. The amount of traffic varies, but it's never too bad. While the riding is certainly pleasant and enjoyable, it's not spectacular. If you want to climb Mt. Diablo, turn north on Mt. Diablo Scenic Blvd.

## Stone Valley Rd./Blackhawk Rd. (Map B)

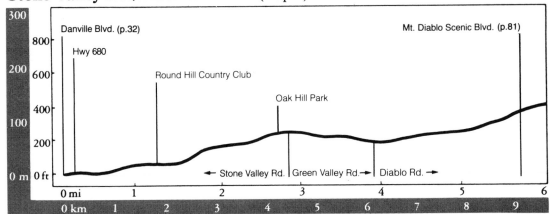

## Stone Valley Rd./Blackhawk Rd. *cont.*

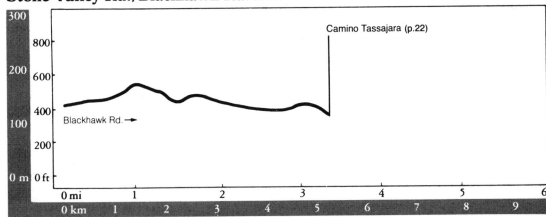

## Summit Rd. (Map B)

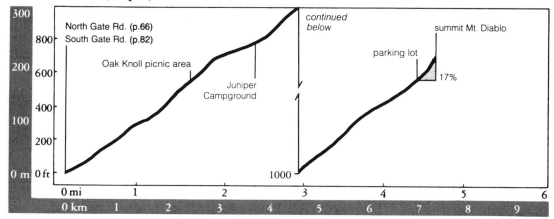

This road to the summit of Mt. Diablo begins about halfway up the mountain. It has an average grade of 6.9%. The last .1 mile is a one-way, very narrow, paved pathway. The view from the top is the second most panoramic in the world (Mt. Kilimanjaro is the first). A snack bar is open seasonally at the top. Call 837-2525 to make sure the park is open; it's often closed during hot, windy periods due to fire hazard.

## Tunnel Rd. (Map A)

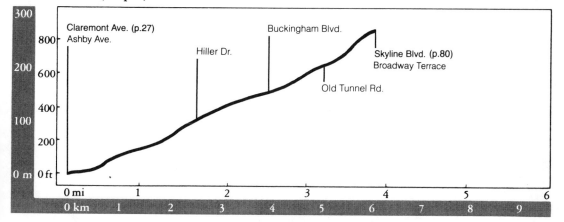

From Claremont Ave. to the signal at Hiller Dr., this has got to be the most nerve-wracking road in California. The extremely heavy traffic during commute hours makes for horrible riding. Between the bottom of Hiller Dr., and Skyline Blvd. it's a wooded, winding road with few houses and little traffic. There's a steady 4.5% grade for the entire road. At Broadway Terrace, Tunnel Rd. becomes Skyline Blvd.

## Upper Happy Valley Rd. (Map A)

A narrow, wooded, residential road in Lafayette. There's a curve at the base of the hill. This road is utilitarian rather than a pure joy. Little traffic.

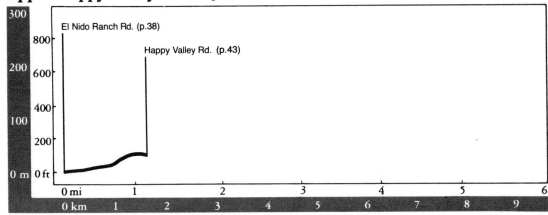

## Vasco Rd. (Maps B,C)

The northernmost 4 miles of this profile are of Walnut Blvd., which becomes Vasco Rd. south of Camino Diablo. South of Hwy 580, it is called South Vasco Rd. For most of its length, this road offers nearly traffic-free riding on a gently winding surface over rolling pasture land. A fun and excellent road, between Brentwood and Livermore.

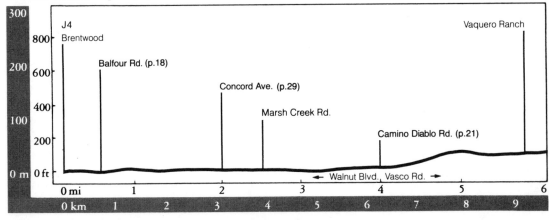

## Vasco Rd. *cont.*

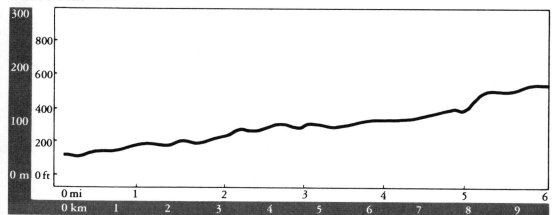

## Vasco Rd. *cont.*

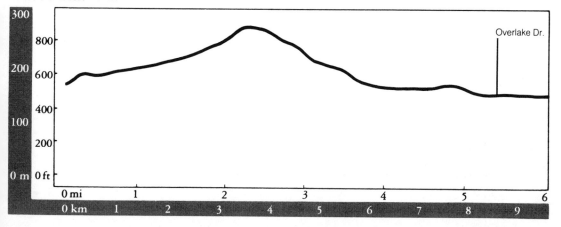

Overlake Dr.

## Vasco Rd. *cont.*

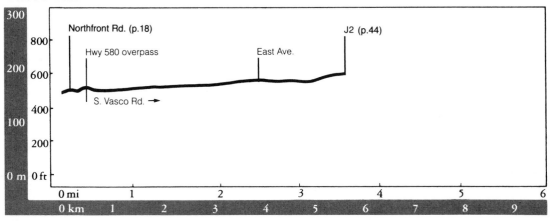

## Wildcat Canyon Rd. (Map A)

A narrow, wooded, winding road. The lower 2.5 miles contain several sharp corners, a few of which are reverse-banked, bumpy, greasy, and have decreasing radii. The westernmost couple of miles are wooded and residential. At various points along the road there are fine views of Wildcat Canyon, distant hills, and San Pablo Reservoir. Inspiration Point is a worthwhile stop.

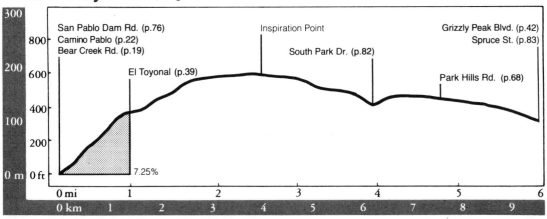

## Ygnacio Valley Rd./Kirker Pass Rd. (Map B)

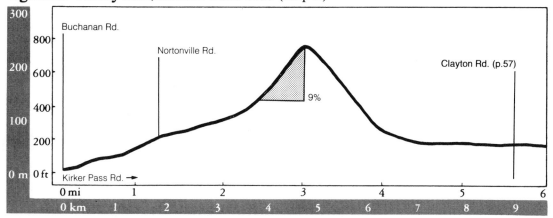

This road travels between eastern Walnut Creek and Pittsburg, and it's no fun at all. There's a lot of heavy traffic and it's not particularly scenic. The least offensive part is the steep hill where there's a little less traffic, a lot of wind, and no businesses lining the road. Clayton Rd. leads to Marsh Creek Rd., which connects with Morgan Territory Rd. and Camino Diablo in eastern Contra Costa County.

## Ygnacio Valley Rd./Kirker Pass Rd. *cont.*

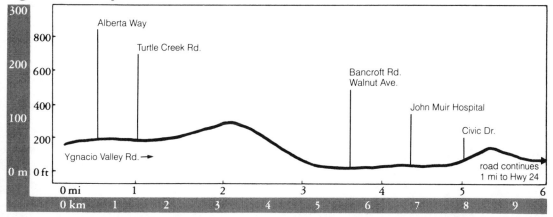

Marshall-Petaluma Rd.

# Marin County

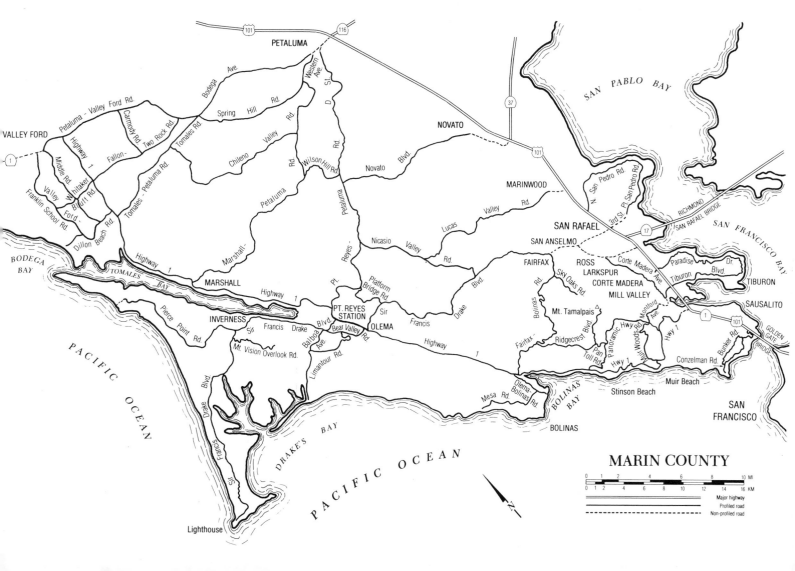

**MARIN COUNTY**

## Balboa Ave.

A narrow, wooded, and very steep residential road that connects Sir Francis Drake Blvd. with Limantour Rd. Very little traffic, no sharp curves.

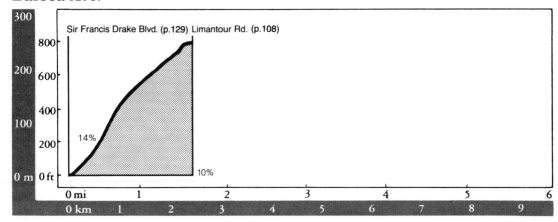

## Bear Valley Rd.

A short, wooded road between Sir Francis Drake Blvd. (near Inverness Park) and Hwy 1 near Olema. It passes the Bear Valley Visitor Center of Pt. Reyes National Seashore.

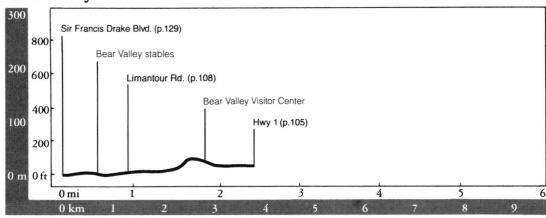

## Bodega Ave.

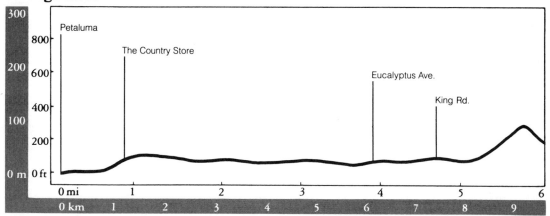

Petaluma

The Country Store

Eucalyptus Ave.

King Rd.

A narrow, well-traveled road through the farm and dairy land between Petaluma and Tomales. The portion closest to Petaluma is more developed than the rest.

## Bodega Ave. *cont.*

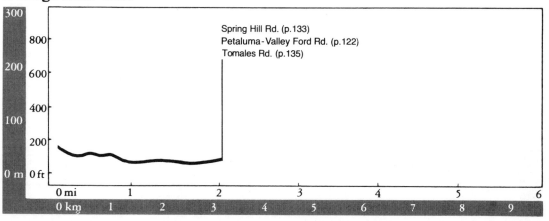

Spring Hill Rd. (p.133)
Petaluma-Valley Ford Rd. (p.122)
Tomales Rd. (p.135)

## Bunker Rd./McCullough Rd.

Bunker Rd. and McCullough Rd. are both fine roads for riding. They travel through the Marin Headlands part of the Golden Gate National Recreation Area, and have only light to moderate car traffic.

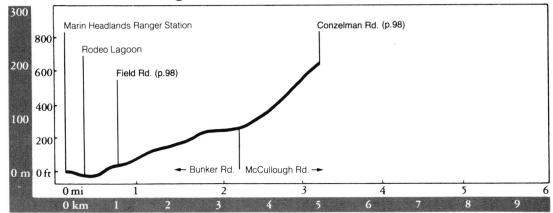

## Carmody Rd.

A short, straight road with a rough surface and no traffic. It travels through pasture land between Fallon-Two Rock Rd. and Petaluma-Valley Ford Rd. in northwestern Marin county. A similar road (Gericke Rd.) parallels this one 3 miles to the west.

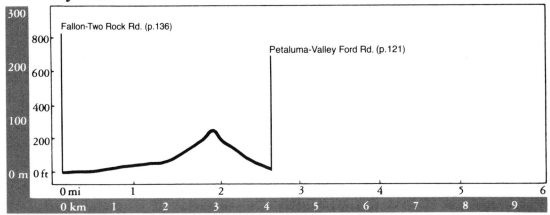

## Chileno Valley Rd.

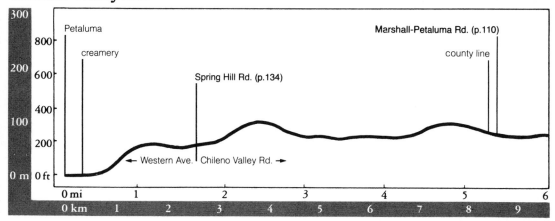

Chileno Valley Rd. and Western Ave. are the same road—the name changes at the Spring Hill Rd. junction, about a mile and a half out of Petaluma. It's a gentle road with excellent riding through flat, rural Chileno Valley. Little traffic.

## Chileno Valley Rd. *cont.*

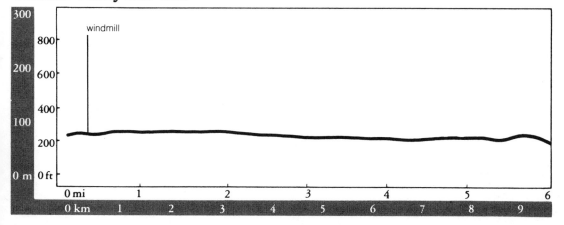

## Chileno Valley Rd. *cont.*

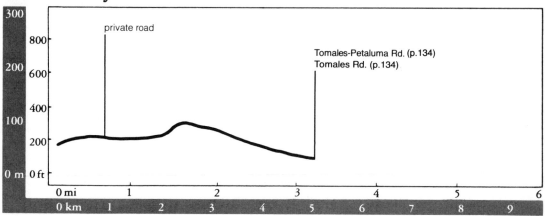

## Conzelman Rd.

Conzelman Rd. travels through the Marin Headlands part of the Golden Gate National Recreation Area. It offers a spectacular ride along the cliffs overlooking the Golden Gate. (Heading north from the Golden Gate Bridge, take the Alexander Ave. exit, then head back south towards S.F.)

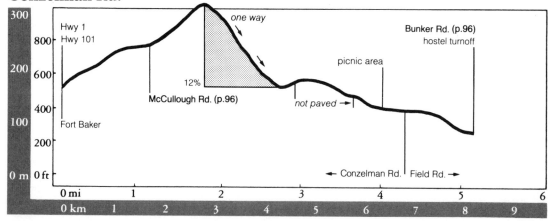

## Corte Madera Ave., etc.

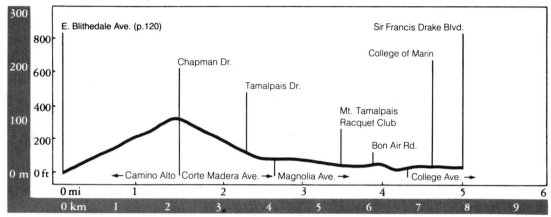

This popular road changes names several times as it runs between E. Blithedale Ave. in Mill Valley and Sir Francis Drake Blvd. in Kentfield. Between E. Blithedale Ave. and Tamalpais Dr. it's a narrow, winding, wooded road. There are few houses; the riding is fun. The northern 2.5-3 miles travel through fairly quiet business districts.

## Dillon Beach Rd.

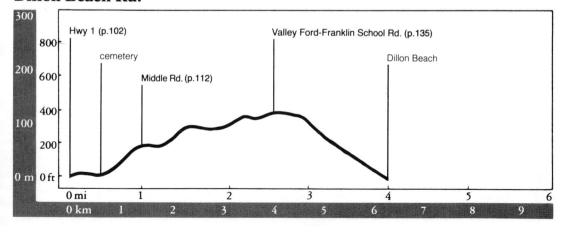

A narrow road that twists over coastal hills in northwestern Marin County between Hwy 1 at Tomales and Bodega Bay. Dillon Beach is popular, and there is bound to be significantly more traffic on this road on summer weekends.

This road is usually closed to motor traffic between Hwy 1 and the Meadow Club Golf Course. The 13 miles between these points are winding, wooded, and beautifully unkempt. The major hills have an average grade of 5.3% in both directions. Many people drive from Fairfax to the locked gate at the Meadow Club and ride from there, thus avoiding some steep, residential climbing. Go south on Ridgecrest Blvd. if you want to ride to the top of Mt. Tamalpais.

## Fairfax-Bolinas Rd.

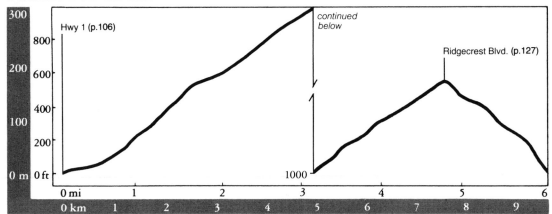

## Fairfax-Bolinas Rd. *cont.*

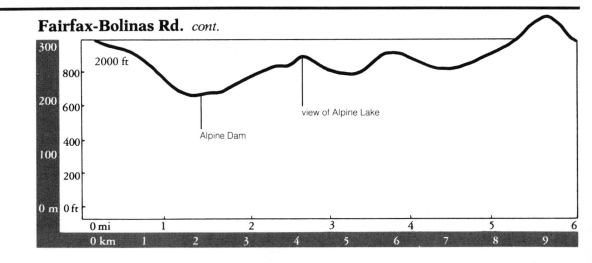

## Fairfax-Bolinas Rd. *cont.*

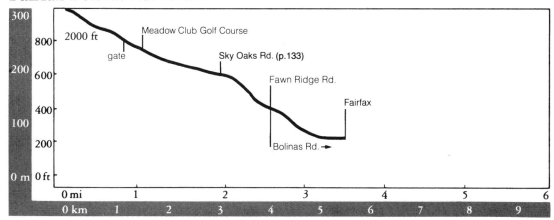

## Highway 1

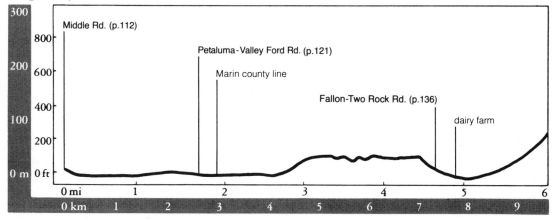

A fun road with a variety of riding conditions—flats, rollers, spectacular climbs. Most of the motor traffic occurs on weekends and is heaviest south of Five Brooks. This profile goes from Valley Ford in Sonoma County to Tamalpais Valley junction in southern Marin County. It passes the entrances to Pt. Reyes National Seashore, Mt. Tamalpais State Park, Stinson Beach, Muir Beach, and the Golden Gate National Recreation Area.

## Highway 1 *cont.*

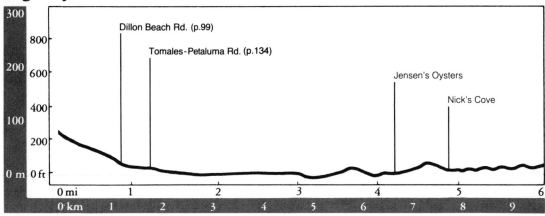

## Highway 1 *cont.*

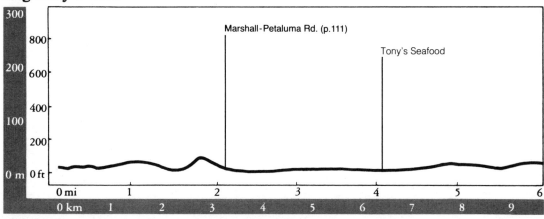

Highway 1

Tomales-Petaluma Rd.

## Highway 1 *cont.*

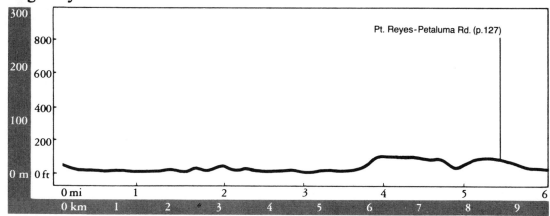

Pt. Reyes-Petaluma Rd. (p.127)

## Highway 1 *cont.*

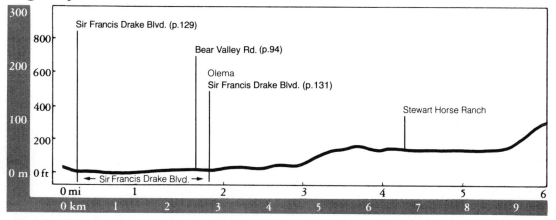

Sir Francis Drake Blvd. (p.129)

Bear Valley Rd. (p.94)

Olema
Sir Francis Drake Blvd. (p.131)

Stewart Horse Ranch

← Sir Francis Drake Blvd. →

## **Highway 1** *cont.*

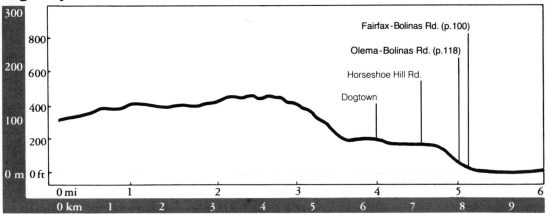

## **Highway 1** *cont.*

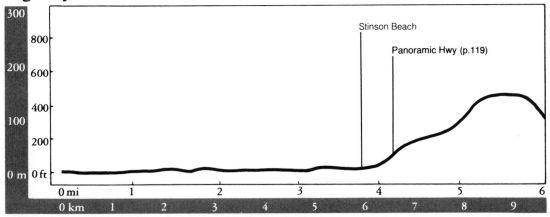

## Highway 1 *cont.*

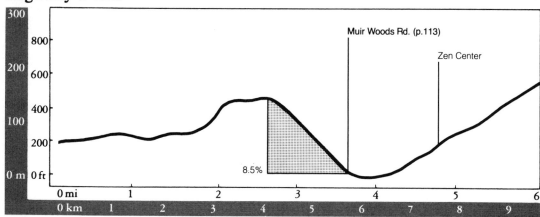

## Highway 1 *cont.*

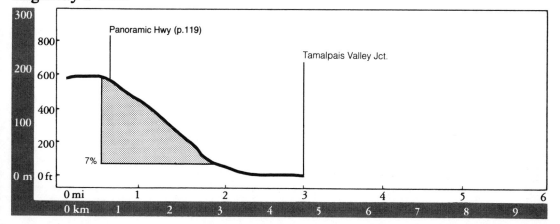

A strenuous and exhilarating road. It travels over brush-covered coastal hills and ends at Limantour Beach. The road was damaged in the flood of 1982, and as of this writing hasn't been repaired. It's currently closed to motor traffic west of Balboa Ave. You can get through with a bicycle, but you'll have to walk it in some places.

## Limantour Rd.

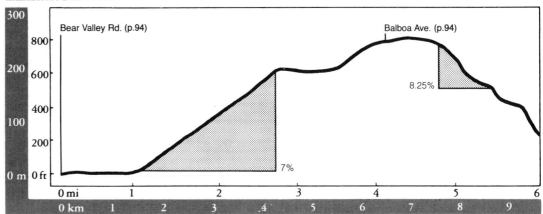

## Limantour Rd. *cont.*

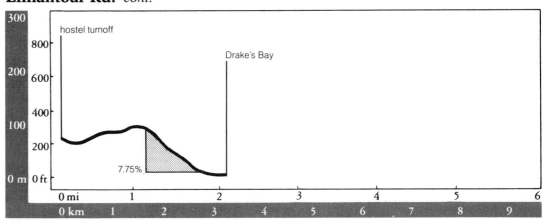

## Lucas Valley Rd.

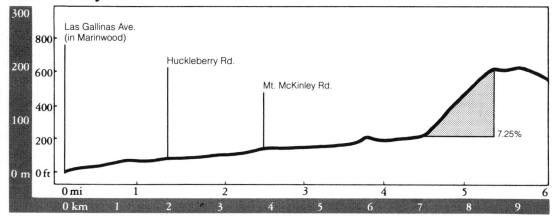

A typically enjoyable inland Marin County road. Near Marinwood it's wide, smooth, and only lightly developed. West of Mt. McKinley Rd. it narrows, becomes more winding and wooded, and less inhabited.

## Lucas Valley Rd. *cont.*

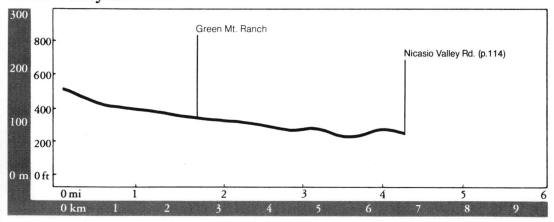

A fine road with a mixture of hills and flats. Much of it parallels a wooded creek through a quiet valley. The false-summitted "Marshall Wall" just off Hwy 1 is the most well-known portion, a prominent feature of the Marin Road Race held each spring.

## Marshall-Petaluma Rd.

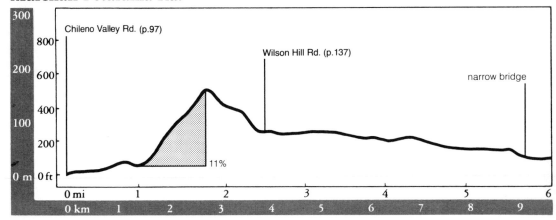

## Marshall-Petaluma Rd. *cont.*

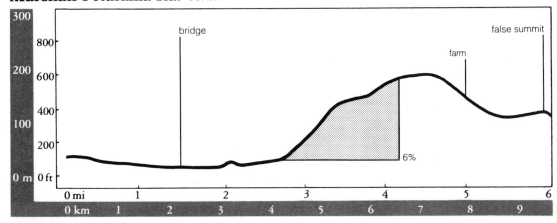

## Marshall-Petaluma Rd. *cont.*

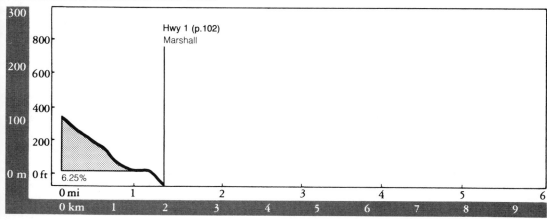

## Mesa Rd.

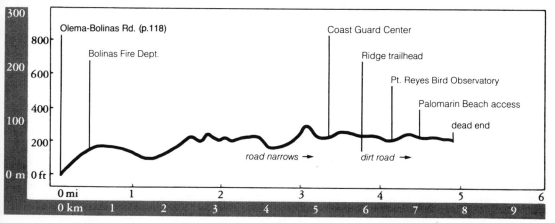

A decent but unspectacular road that travels between Olema-Bolinas Rd. (just outside Bolinas) and Palomarin Beach. On the way you'll pass a trailhead and—probably the best reason for riding this road —the Pt. Reyes Bird Observatory (visitors welcome). The last 1.25-mile stretch is unpaved. Little traffic.

## Middle Rd.

This must be named Middle Rd. because it parallels and runs midway between Valley Ford-Franklin School Rd. (to the west) and Hwy 1 (to the east). A fun, quiet, skinny road in pretty country.

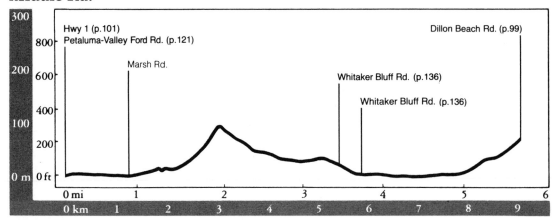

## Montford Ave., etc.

This is a popular shortcut between Miller Ave. in Mill Valley and Panoramic Hwy on the western edge of Mt. Tamalpais State Park. It's narrow and winding with a bumpy surface. The road travels through a wooded residential area and has an average grade of 5.5%, although a few short pitches are considerably steeper.

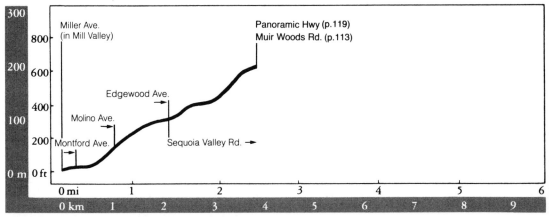

## Mount Vision Overlook Rd.

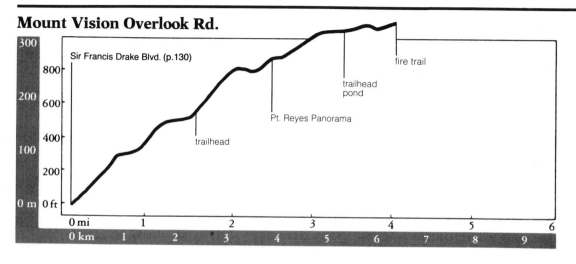

Sir Francis Drake Blvd. (p.130)

trailhead

Pt. Reyes Panorama

trailhead
pond

fire trail

This is an extremely narrow road with an abrasive (but not bumpy) surface. It heads south from Sir Francis Drake Blvd. a few miles west of Inverness, and hairpins its way over the slopes of Mt. Vision. It ends at a fire trail on the northwestern side of Pt. Reyes Hill. There is a great view from the Pt. Reyes Panorama turnout. Up to the Pt. Reyes Panorama the average grade is 6.25%, but as the profile shows, it is not a constant grade.

## Muir Woods Rd.

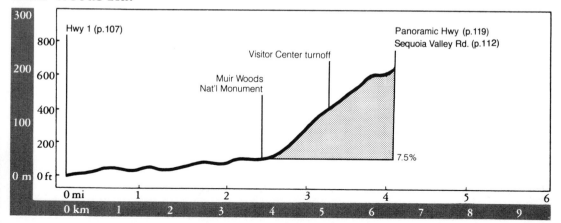

Hwy 1 (p.107)

Panoramic Hwy (p.119)
Sequoia Valley Rd. (p.112)

Visitor Center turnoff

Muir Woods
Nat'l Monument

7.5%

A winding, wooded road that becomes hilly and travels through Frank Valley in the southeastern portion of Mt. Tamalpais State Park. It's something of a shortcut between Hwy 1 and Panoramic Hwy (at Sequoia Valley Rd.). From this junction, it's a quick 2.5 mile descent into Mill Valley.

## Nicasio Valley Rd.

For most of its length, this is a flat, quiet road through the wide Nicasio valley. The road surface is fine and the traffic is light.

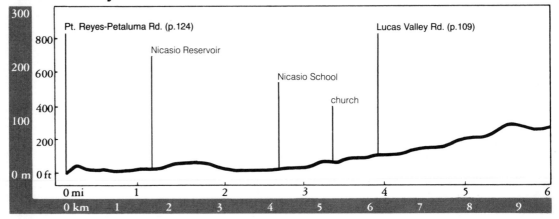

## Nicasio Valley Rd. *cont.*

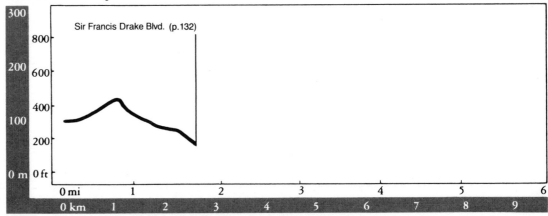

Valley Ford-Franklin School Rd.

Wilson Hill Rd.

## Novato Blvd.

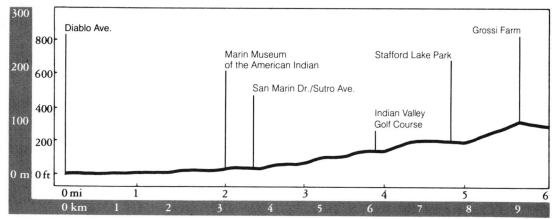

Except for the developed couple of miles nearest Diablo Ave. in downtown Novato, this is a fine, narrow, lightly-trafficked road through pasture land.

## Novato Blvd. *cont.*

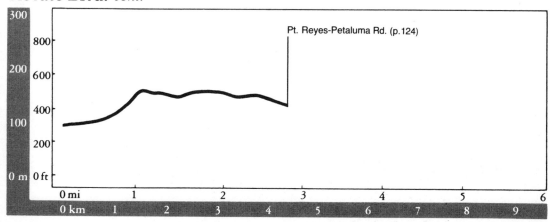

## Olema-Bolinas Rd.

A narrow, wooded road that runs alongside the western shore of Bolinas Lagoon, joining Hwy 1 with the town of Bolinas. Despite its name, it does not go to Olema, but begins about 9 miles south of that town, near the western end of Fairfax-Bolinas Rd.

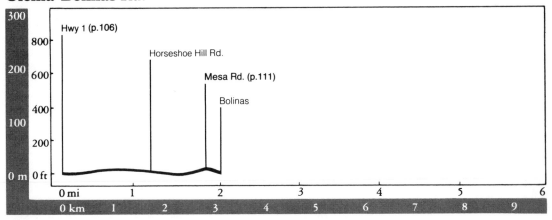

## Pan Toll Rd.

A short connector between Panoramic Hwy and Ridgecrest Blvd., and similar in character to both of these roads. It's narrow and wooded. Also known as Southside Rd.

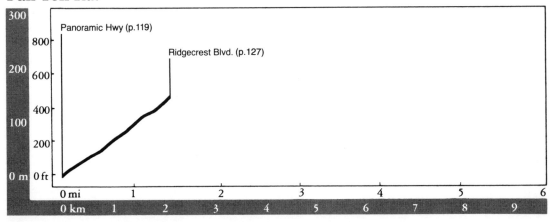

## Panoramic Highway

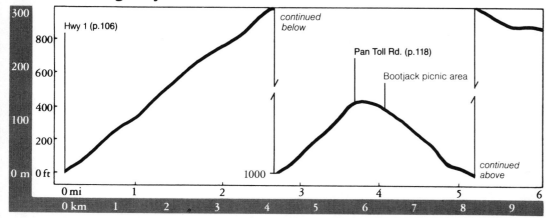

This is a winding, brushy, and fairly narrow road with a fine surface and excellent riding. The views it provides are indeed "panoramic," which accounts for its popularity with motorists as well as bicyclists. The road travels through Mt. Tamalpais State Park. From Hwy 1 to Pan Toll Rd. it has an average grade of 7.25%.

## Panoramic Highway *cont.*

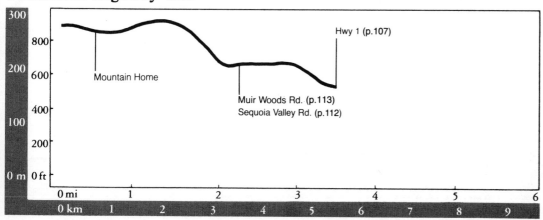

This is a popular ride around the Tiburon peninsula. It begins as E. Blithedale Ave. on the eastern edge of Mill Valley and passes through about 5 miles of small business districts and the town of Tiburon. Paradise Dr. itself is narrow, twisty, and lined with trees.

## Paradise Dr./Tiburon Blvd.

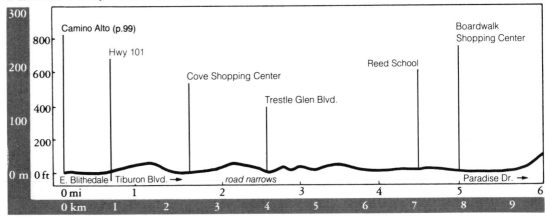

## Paradise Dr./Tiburon Blvd. *cont.*

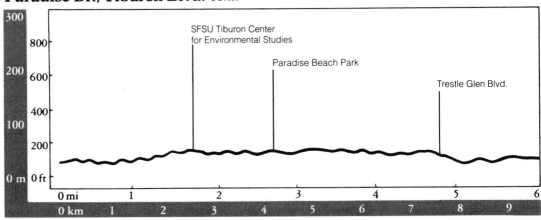

## Paradise Dr./Tiburon Blvd. *cont.*

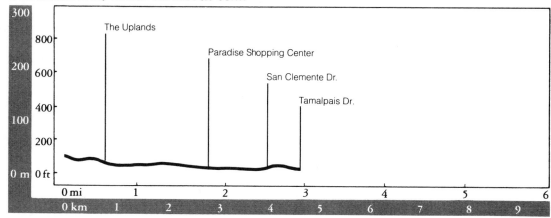

## Petaluma-Valley Ford Rd.

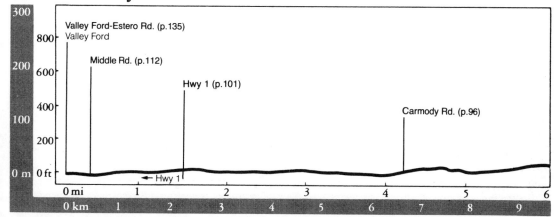

A fairly typical inland Marin County road—rural and relatively flat. This one has more traffic than the smaller roads in the area since it travels between Petaluma and Valley Ford.

## Petaluma-Valley Ford Rd. *cont.*

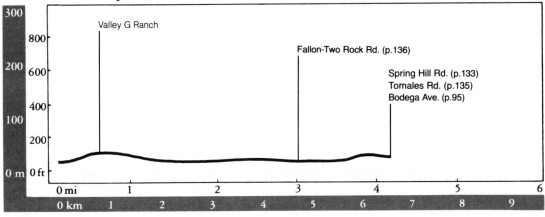

## Pierce Point Rd.

Particularly enjoyable if you don't have to contend with weekend traffic. Much like the western portion of Sir Francis Drake Blvd., it climbs and descends the pastoral hills of Pt. Reyes National Seashore and ends at the coast.

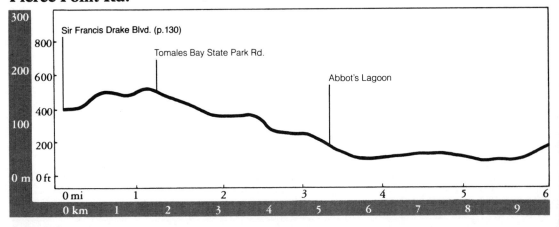

## Pierce Point Rd. *cont.*

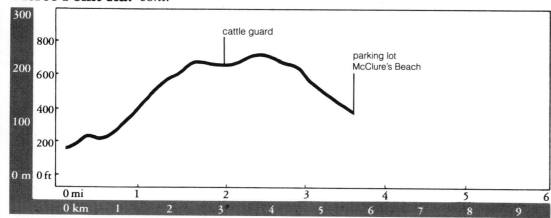

cattle guard

parking lot
McClure's Beach

## Platform Bridge Rd.

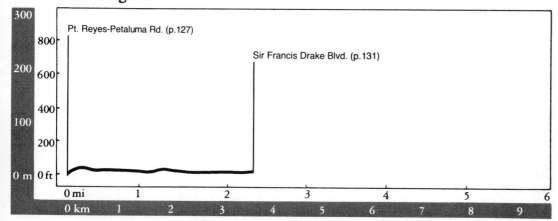

Pt. Reyes-Petaluma Rd. (p.127)

Sir Francis Drake Blvd. (p.131)

A useful connector between
Pt. Reyes-Petaluma Rd. and
Sir Francis Drake Blvd. It
parallels Paper Mill Creek and
borders Bolinas Ridge. Narrow,
lightly travelled, wooded.

## Pt. Reyes-Petaluma Rd.

The northeastern portion of this road is in Sonoma County, where it is called D St. The section between Petaluma and The Cheese Factory is also known as Red Hill Rd. It's a typical inland Marin County road, traveling through mostly gently rolling pastures. The Marin French Cheese Company ("The Cheese Factory") is a popular stop. You can buy cheese, eat it at picnic tables under shade trees, and watch ducks in the pond.

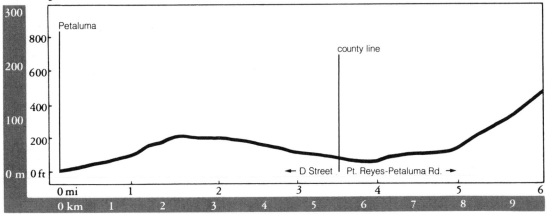

## Pt. Reyes-Petaluma Rd. *cont.*

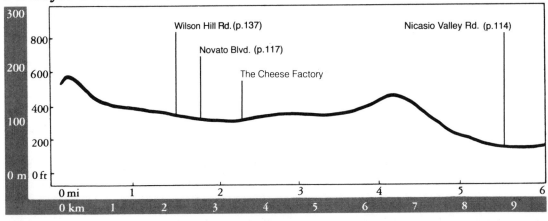

Panoramic Highway

Point Reyes-Petaluma Rd.

## Pt. Reyes-Petaluma Rd. *cont.*

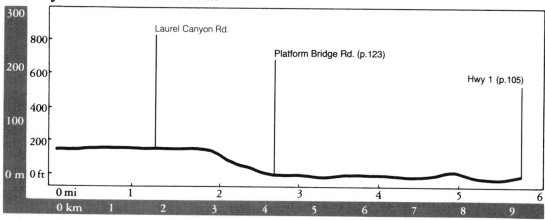

## Ridgecrest Blvd.

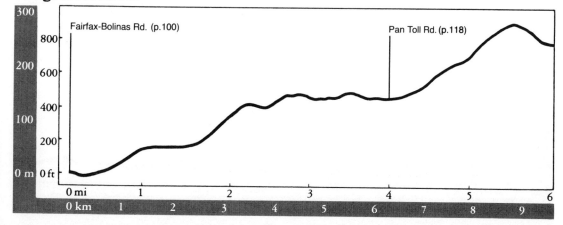

This road begins at the summit of Fairfax-Bolinas Rd. It travels southeast along Bolinas Ridge in a series of long, rolling climbs, with excellent views of Bolinas Bay to the west and distant hills to the east. At Pan Toll junction the road turns north and begins the main climb to the top of Mt. Tamalpais. This part is more wooded and winding and narrower than the lower, more exposed section. Average grade for the entire road is 3.3%.

## Ridgecrest Blvd. *cont.*

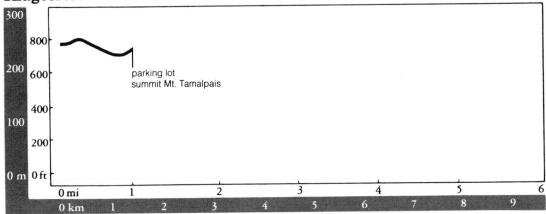

parking lot
summit Mt. Tamalpais

## San Pedro Rd., North/Pt. San Pedro Rd.

This is a basically flat, gently winding road east of San Rafael. It goes around the point of land that separates San Pablo Bay from San Francisco Bay, passing through China Camp State Park and McNears Beach County Park. Pleasant but unchallenging.

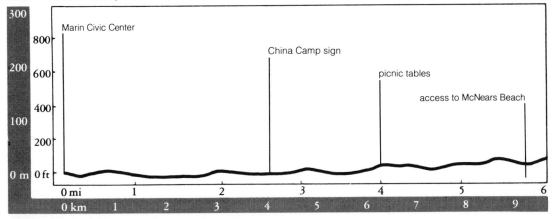

Marin Civic Center

China Camp sign

picnic tables

access to McNears Beach

## San Pedro Rd., North/Pt. San Pedro Rd. *cont.*

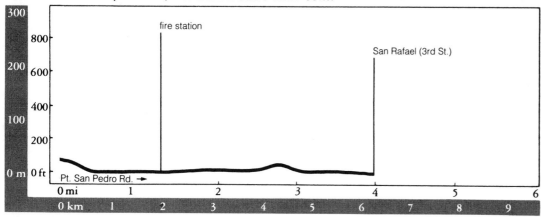

## Sir Francis Drake Blvd. (Pt. Reyes Station to Lighthouse)

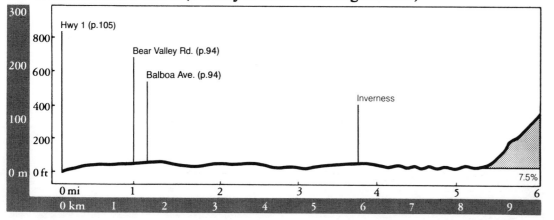

This is a narrow road that rolls through the coastal hills and pasture land in Pt. Reyes National Seashore. During December and January, when the whales are migrating, the weekend traffic can be stifling. You're still better off on a bicycle, though, since you'll be able to ride around the often mile-long line of waiting motorists. Other times the traffic is light and the riding excellent.

## Sir Francis Drake Blvd. (Pt. Reyes Station to Lighthouse) *cont.*

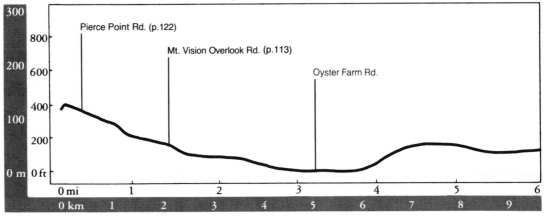

Pierce Point Rd. (p.122)

Mt. Vision Overlook Rd. (p.113)

Oyster Farm Rd.

## Sir Francis Drake Blvd. (Pt. Reyes Station to Lighthouse) *cont.*

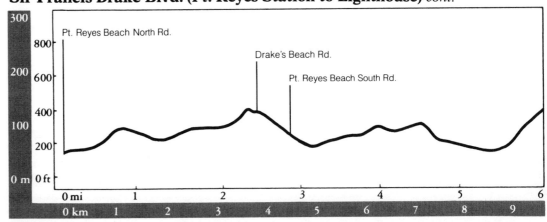

Pt. Reyes Beach North Rd.

Drake's Beach Rd.

Pt. Reyes Beach South Rd.

## Sir Francis Drake Blvd. (Pt. Reyes Station to Lighthouse) *cont.*

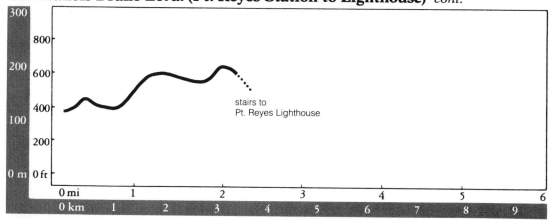

stairs to
Pt. Reyes Lighthouse

## Sir Francis Drake Blvd. (Olema to Fairfax)

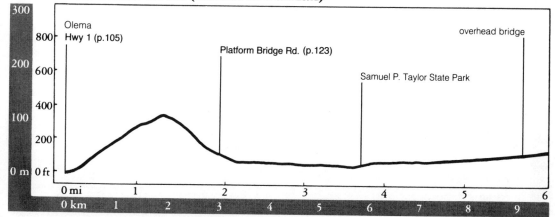

Olema
Hwy 1 (p.105)

Platform Bridge Rd. (p.123)

overhead bridge

Samuel P. Taylor State Park

Just inland from Olema, Sir Francis Drake Blvd. climbs a large, shadeless hill with a rough surface. The portion through Samuel P. Taylor State Park is narrow, winding, and densely wooded. Between Lagunitas and Fairfax the road widens, the surface improves, and it becomes more urban. East of Fairfax (not on these profiles), use the bike trails, as there's too much motor traffic on the main road.

## Sir Francis Drake Blvd. (Olema to Fairfax) *cont.*

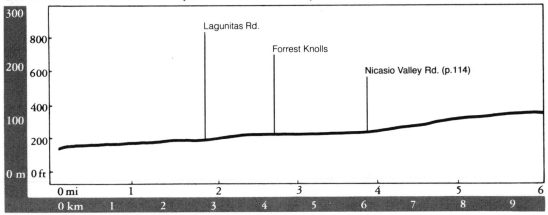

## Sir Francis Drake Blvd. (Olema to Fairfax) *cont.*

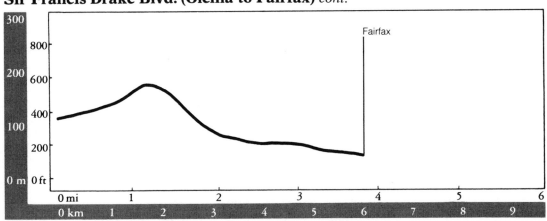

## Sky Oaks Rd./Lagunitas Lake Rd.

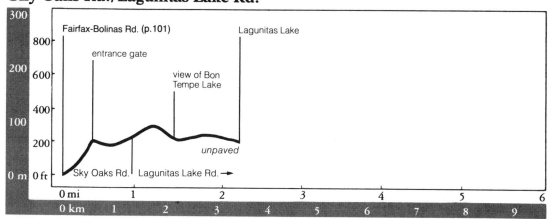

Sky Oaks Rd., also called the Old Bolinas-Fairfax Rd., is a very narrow, wooded road with a particularly rough surface. It heads south from the Fairfax-Bolinas Rd., about 1.75 miles out of Fairfax. After about .9 mile, you'll come to a fork in the road. If you turn right, you'll go to Bon Tempe lake. If you turn left, as the profile does, the road will take you to Lagunitas Lake on an extremely windy, narrow, and wooded road.

## Spring Hill Rd.

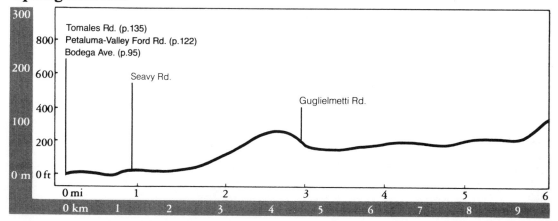

A quiet, rural road in southern Sonoma County. It travels through farm country, and has a rough surface and almost no traffic.

## Spring Hill Rd. *cont.*

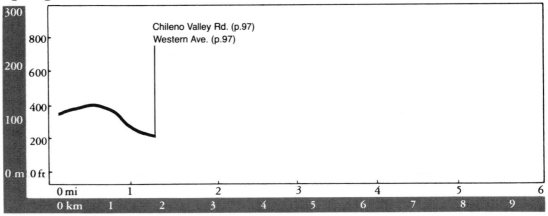

## Tomales-Petaluma Rd.

This road travels through the dairy land of northwestern Marin County. It's fairly straight, gentle, and mostly unshaded, with light traffic.

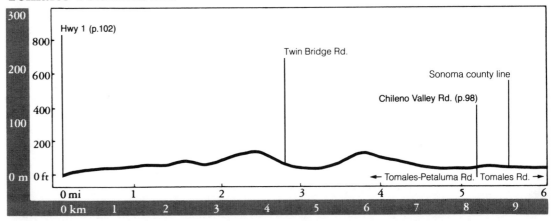

## Tomales-Petaluma Rd. *cont.*

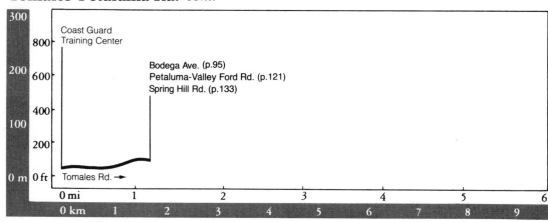

## Valley Ford-Franklin School Rd.

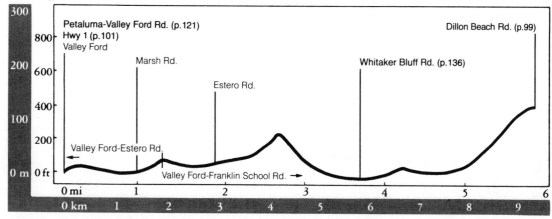

These two connecting roads are in the northwestern corner of Marin County. This is an especially fun ride, interesting and pretty, with very little traffic.

## Whitaker Bluff Rd./Fallon-Two Rock Rd.

A couple of basically flat, rural roads in northwestern Marin County. The riding is pleasant, the traffic is light. The quality of the road's surface changes drastically at the county line.

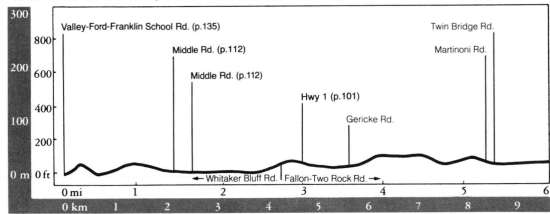

## Whitaker Bluff Rd./Fallon-Two Rock Rd. *cont.*

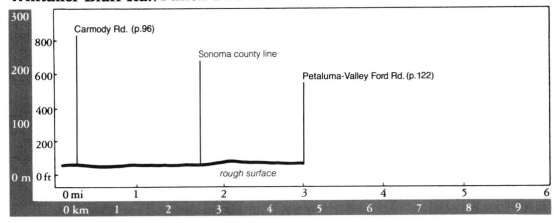

## Wilson Hill Rd.

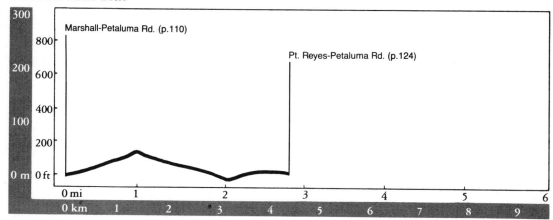

Despite its name, this road has no significant hill. It's an inland road through pasture land, and connects Marshall-Petaluma Rd. with Pt. Reyes-Petaluma Rd.

Lucas Valley Rd.

## BART

You can take your bike on BART just once without a *BART Bicycle Permit*. If you want a permit, write for an application. The address is:

BART Bicycle Permit
800 Madison Street
Oakland, CA 94607

or phone (415) 465-4100, x569

The cost is $3.00 and the permit is good for 3 years. When you get your permit you'll also receive a sheet of rules and bicycle–legal hours.

## Bridges

*Richmond-San Rafael Bridge*:
No riding allowed. A privately owned public service called *Traveler's Transit* runs a van (with room for two bikes) between the Richmond BART station and downtown San Rafael. It makes 11 round trips each weekday, and 5 on weekends and holidays. The cost is $2.00 per person and 25¢ per bicycle. For a schedule and more information, call Traveler's Transit in San Rafael at (415) 457-7080.

*S.F.-Oakland Bay Bridge*:
No riding allowed. On weekdays during no-bike hours on BART, Caltrans operates a bicycle/rider shuttle between the MacArthur BART station and Main St. at Folsom in San Francisco. It costs 50¢ and it can carry 12 bikes. The shuttle does not operate on weekends. For more information, call (415) 557-1611.

*Golden Gate Bridge*:
Bicycle riding allowed on the sidewalks. On weekdays you must stay on the east sidewalk; on weekends and holidays the west. Bicycle-legal hours are 6 a.m. to 9 p.m. on weekdays. On weekends the bridge is closed to bicycle traffic after sunset. For more information, call (415) 921-5828.

*Hayward-San Mateo Bridge*:
No riding allowed. You can be shuttled across on a Caltrans maintenance vehicle providing it isn't needed for official use, but you must make arrangements 24 hours in advance. Phone Caltrans at (415) 464-0876 or 464-0699 for more information.

*Antioch Bridge*:
No riding.

*Carquinez Straits Bridge*:
No riding.

*Benicia-Martinez Bridge*:
No riding.

*Dumbarton Bridge*:
Riding allowed in the bike lane.

## Ferries

You can take your bicycle free on the following ferries. The information was current as of November 1983, but a telephone call will provide the latest schedule and fare information.

*Sausalito Ferry*:
*Time*: About 30 minutes
*Route*: Sausalito Point (downtown Sausalito) to the Ferry Building at the end of Market St. in S.F. (for the *Golden Gate Transit* ferry). Sausalito Point to Pier 41 (Fisherman's Wharf Ferry Terminal) (for the *Red & White Fleet* ferry).
*Telephone*: 453-2100 (Marin Co.); 332-6600 (S.F. *Golden Gate Transit*); 546-2815 (*Red & White Fleet*).

*Larkspur Ferry*:
*Time*: 45-55 minutes
*Route*: Larkspur Landing (east of Highway 101, opposite the Greenbrae turnoff) to the Ferry Building in S.F.
*Telephone*: 453-2100 (Marin Co.); 332-6600 (S.F. *Golden Gate Transit*).

*Tiburon Ferry*:
*Time*: weekdays 30 minutes; weekends 40-50 minutes.
*Route*: Main St. Wharf in Tiburon to north side of Ferry Building in S.F.
*Telephone*: 546-2815 (*Red & White Fleet*)

*Tiburon/Angel Island Ferry*:
*Time*: **10 minutes (Tiburon-Angel Island); 35 minutes (Angel Island-S.F.)**
*Route*: **Main St. Wharf in Tiburon to Angel Island to Pier 43½ (Fisherman's Wharf) in S.F.**
*Telephone*: 546-2815 (*Red & White Fleet*).
Labor Day through May 31 there is weekend and holiday service *only*.